How to Make
CLAY CHARACTERS

How to Make
CLAY
Characters

MAUREEN CARLSON

WITHDRAWN

NORTH LIGHT BOOKS

Cincinnati, Ohio

ABOUT THE AUTHOR

Maureen Carlson is a teacher, writer, designer and storyteller. The common thread in all of these areas is the oven-baked polymer clay from which she creates her whimsical characters.

Maureen says that if her life were written like a fairy tale, it would begin . . .

. . . Once upon a time there was a little pigtailed girl who lived on a Michigan dairy farm amongst the cats and the cows, and who spent her days building things to play with from blocks of wood, leftover vegetables from the garden and scraps of fabric.

When she grew up she traded the farm for a job as an elementary teacher and then life as a "creative" wife and mother. Diapers and flower gardens, church meetings and organizational opportunities, outdoor craft shows and serendipitous books and acquaintances were all thrown into the life pot and stirred with enthusiasm and persistence. Twenty years later, she one day found herself to be an expert in polymer clay.

Maureen has written books for Hot Off the Press, has produced five instructional videos and has written for numerous craft publications. In 1995, she was named "Craft Designer of the Year" in a contest sponsored by Loctite Corporation and *Craft and Needlework Age* magazine. Her line of collectible figures, Pippsywoggins, Little Friends From The Edge Of Imagination, can be found at gift stores nationwide.

Maureen and her husband Dan, have two grown daughters who frequently visit the rural home in Minnesota where she survives the stress of deadlines by digging in her gardens.

Other fine North Light Books are available from your local bookstore, art supply store or direct from the publisher.

01 00 99 98 97   5 4 3 2 1

Library of Congress Cataloging-in-Publication Data

Carlson, Maureen.
    How to make clay characters / Maureen Carlson.
        p.   cm.
    Includes index.
    ISBN 0-89134-721-6
    1. Polymer clay craft. I. Title.
TT297.C28 1997
731.4′2—dc20   96-38418
                                  CIP

Edited by Kathy Kipp and Jennifer Long
Production Edited by Michelle Kramer
Cover designed by Angela Lennert Wilcox
Chapter opener photographs by Lloyd H. Wilson

North Light Books are available for sales promotions, premiums and fund-raising use. Special editions or book excerpts can also be created to specification. For details contact: Special Sales Manager, F&W Publications, 1507 Dana Avenue, Cincinnati, Ohio 45207.

METRIC CONVERSION CHART		
TO CONVERT	**TO**	**MULTIPLY BY**
Inches	Centimeters	2.54
Centimeters	Inches	0.4
Feet	Centimeters	30.5
Centimeters	Feet	0.03
Yards	Meters	0.9
Meters	Yards	1.1
Sq. Inches	Sq. Centimeters	6.45
Sq. Centimeters	Sq. Inches	0.16
Sq. Feet	Sq. Meters	0.09
Sq. Meters	Sq. Feet	10.8
Sq. Yards	Sq. Meters	0.8
Sq. Meters	Sq. Yards	1.2
Pounds	Kilograms	0.45
Kilograms	Pounds	2.2
Ounces	Grams	28.4
Grams	Ounces	0.04

DEDICATION

Dedicated to my mother, AnaBel Peck, who stole moments away from the weeding and canning and scrubbing that come with life on a farm to take us on walks through the woods, to the library and to lectures given by local celebrities (of which she was one). Because of her, I hold in awe the feel, the smell and the magic of books.

ACKNOWLEDGMENTS

Without the calm reassurance of editor Kathy Kipp, this book would not have happened. About three-fourths of the way through, I felt like I had surrounded myself with such a pile of papers and pictures and samples and patterns that the only way out was to lie down and go to sleep! Kathy wouldn't let that happen, and we both "kept on dancin'." Thanks to content editor Jennifer Long, who brought the same air of calm and encouragement to her part of the job. And to my husband, Dan—who believes that I can do anything I want to do, and who gives me the support to do it—I give a big smile of appreciation.

TABLE OF CONTENTS

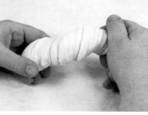

My first memory of polymer clay is from the year 1975 or 1976. In the memory I see myself sitting at the kitchen table in our Mentor, Ohio, home showing a neighbor my latest creation— a stick from the yard onto which I had sculpted a climbing boy. I'm sure it was crude, as my skills were minimal. But I remember my neighbor's reaction: surprise and pleasure at the image I had created, and enthusiasm and encouragement for me.

Eventually, I turned the making of clay characters into a family business. Yet, it is that first enthusiastic memory that symbolizes for me the key elements that make polymer clay such a delightful material:

▶ *It's easy to find.*

▶ *No special equipment is required.*

▶ *No special training is needed to begin.*

▶ *Its uses are unlimited.*

▶ *The finished creation is durable and long-lasting.*

▶ *It meets the needs of both beginners and professionals.*

My first request as you begin this book is that you relax and enjoy the process of creative play. Don't worry about getting the first figures "just right." Being able to impart a mood and a character to your pieces can happen even if your skills are still rough. Expertise, just as with any art medium, will come as you practice and gain skill in controlling the clay. The first thing to do is to just create—like a child playing with a new box of crayons. As you begin to learn tricks for making the clay do what you want, you will have more and more success at bringing to life the characters that dwell within your imagination.

I began teaching classes in 1984 in response to requests from my customers at the Minnesota Renaissance Festival. At first I was amazed at how quickly people picked up my hints and shortcut steps for creating characters. Since then, I have learned to expect the unexpected from my students. And I have found that they continually stretch and teach me through their eagerness to find new ways to express their creativity. It is with this spirit that I write this book. I share with you what I have learned, knowing that you can take that knowledge and improve on it. Show me what you can do. Amaze me.

CHAPTER ONE

Choosing Your Clay

The colors and varieties of polymer clays now on the market are so wonderful that, even if you never get around to making anything more than a color-swirled snake, it would be worth buying some just to experiment with mixing colors and creating simple shapes. Here is a quick reference guide to help you decide which brand of clay is right for your first project.

GENERAL CHARACTERISTICS

Polymer clays all have the same basic structure. They are compounds made of polyvinyl chloride (PVC) mixed with a plasticizer for flexibility, a filler for texture and pigments for color.

As you read this book, you will notice that I refer to polymer clay simply as clay, even though it is man-made and not a naturally occurring clay. It does, however, have many of the same qualities as the natural clays used for ceramics—polymer clays can be molded, sculpted, rolled and imprinted. But, unlike the ceramic clays (which require high-temperature firing in a kiln), the polymer clays harden permanently in a regular home oven.

Polymer clay is extremely heat sensitive. It softens when subjected to low heat, such as that of a warm human hand, while it hardens, permanently, when heated to between

200° F and 275° F. It will also begin to harden, even in the package, if it is stored or shipped improperly. Polymer clay should be stored and shipped at temperatures less than 100° F, and should be kept out of direct sunlight. (I have not noticed any harm caused by freezing polymer clay, either baked or unbaked.)

Due to the heat sensitivity of the polymer clays, when testing out a brand it's wise to test several packages purchased at different times from different sources. Not all packages are the same. Age also seems to be a factor in the condition of the clay. Although I have almost always been able to condition old packages of clay by adding a softener, such as Mix Quick or Friendly Clay Super Softener, and mixing it in my food processor, you can avoid the "curse of the hard clay" altogether by purchasing polymer clay that is less than two years old.

After baking, polymer clay can be drilled, carved, sanded and polished. It can be baked in stages, and can be rebaked—though each additional baking will tend to darken the colors. Since polymer clay is a plastic compound, it never becomes completely rigid, even after long baking, so expect it to feel slightly flexible. In fact, some brands, such as ProMat, emphasize their flexibility as a marketing feature.

CHOOSING A BRAND OF POLYMER CLAY

When I am choosing which clay to use for a project, I consider cost, package consistency (how hard or soft the clay is straight out of the wrapper), working consistency (whether the clay becomes very soft or remains firm after being warmed and kneaded by hand), finished strength and flexibility, and available colors.

I have been using the German polymer clay, FIMO, since 1979. Because of my familiarity with it, it is usually my clay of choice for little characters. However, I keep all of the major polymer clays currently on the U.S. market in my supply cabinet, often using two or three different brands in one project.

Any of the following brands will work for the projects in this book. Each brand does have its own qualities, however, so just because a brand will work does not mean it is the ideal one for you to use. Also, keep in mind that polymer clays are relatively new products, and as such are always in the process of change. Expect to see exciting developments in both current brands and new market entries in the near future.

CERNIT

Manufactured in Germany, Cernit is best known for the translucent wax-like finish it gives to dolls. It is also very strong when baked, making it suitable for items that will be handled. Although the flesh tones are most widely recognized, the colors are also wonderful, with glistening glamour tones and subtle, transparent hues. The color of Cernit will change during the baking process due to its translucency; however, this can be alleviated by adding a small amount of opaque white to all the colors.

Cernit is very receptive to warm working conditions—even the heat of your hand. A fresh package will get very soft during the sculpting process. This can be either a help or a hindrance, depending on your working style. Since I do a lot of reworking and hand-holding of my pieces, I find new Cernit too soft for small sculptures.

FIMO

Made by Eberhard Faber in Germany, this clay tends to be very hard and crumbly when first opened. This discourages many users, though the problem can be reduced by taking the time to warm it before starting to knead. Once FIMO is warm and well kneaded, or conditioned, it is firm enough to allow for repetitive handling, yet flexible enough for easy shaping. This makes it perfect for the draping techniques in this book. If FIMO is too stiff for you, alter it by adding the soft kneading medium Mix Quick, which is manufactured for this purpose. (Softening techniques are discussed in the next chapter.)

FIMO SOFT

A relatively new product, FIMO Soft, was developed for people who need an immediately usable clay—in other words, soft from the package. I recommend it for children and beginning users, or for those with hand problems. For detailed and delicate work, I find any of the soft clays more difficult to use.

Because of its rigid strength, Cernit is well suited for making large items like this 22″ doll I made as a graduation gift for my daughter.

This fairy is resting on a stone pile made from FIMO stone colors. FIMO is my clay of choice for beginners, as its stiff consistency tends to forgive overhandling. Its major drawback is it's tendency to be hard to condition.

FRIENDLY CLAY

Manufactured by American Art Clay Company, Inc., this clay first came on the market in 1993. It is slightly softer than FIMO, though still firm. Once conditioned, it does not get softer with continued use. Care must be taken when attaching parts together, as extra pressure must be applied to create a firm bond. Friendly Clay works well for the projects in this book. If it seems hard to you, regulate its consistency by adding Friendly Clay Super Softener.

PROMAT

ProMat, Sculpey (Polyform), Sculpey III, Super Sculpey and Granitex are all manufactured in the United States by the Polyform Company. ProMat is a moderately soft, very strong clay. It is quite flexible when baked, making it excellent for creating wispy hair, flowing garments and decorative elements such as ropes and bracelets. It works well for the projects in this book, especially those where fine detail would be too fragile for the other clays. If you wish to create a rigid sculpture, you may find its flexibility unsettling. A little Super Sculpey can be added to some packages of ProMat to soften them to a drapable consistency. (Don't automatically add it, however, as ProMat seems stiff when cold, but gets soft when warm.)

SCULPEY

Sculpey is a soft clay that comes only in white. It is not very strong, but is good for models that require bulk, as it is the most inexpensive polymer clay. Many artists use it for sculpting their production masters or for items that will be painted. Because of its chalky texture and weakness, I don't recommend it for the projects in this book. Both Sculpey and Super Sculpey scorch easily with repetitive oven bakings.

Friendly Clay is a firm clay that drapes and handles well once it is thoroughly conditioned. Both Friendly Clay and FIMO offer premade millefiori canes that can be sliced and used for patterned accents.

ProMat is a very strong, flexible clay that is frequently used for jewelry production. I use ProMat when making very fragile items, such as this grandmother's hair.

SCULPEY III

This is a very soft clay that comes in many colors, including metallics and brilliants. It is valued for its package consistency by those who require a soft clay. This initial softness has made Sculpey III a favorite of children and beginners. It also has a wonderful matte finish that, to me, is less plastic-looking than the other colored polymer clays. Because it's not very durable when used for thin sheets and delicate detailing, I don't recommend it for my particular figure-making techniques. But if you alter my patterns to create thicker, chunkier designs, its soft consistency may be attractive to you. You'll need to learn to hold it lightly, as the soft clays fingerprint very easily.

SUPER SCULPEY

This form of Sculpey is a very soft clay that comes only in a pink/beige color. It is a favorite of dollmakers and origi-nal model sculptors due to its easy workability and strength. Many artists extend and soften their FIMO by mixing it with Super Sculpey. For this book, Super Sculpey can be used for the skin areas, for mixing with FIMO colors to soften them and for armatures.

SAFETY PRECAUTIONS

All major polymer clays on the market have been certified nontoxic when used according to manufacturers' directions. When using a new brand, always check the package for the *AP NONTOXIC* label. It's true that since these are plastic materials, any baking of the polymer clays will result in an odor. But, while these odors may be unpleasant, they should not be harmful. Use adequate ventilation if you find these smells offensive.

The acrid smoke of burning polymer clays is another matter. These fumes may cause irritation to your breathing passages. The danger zone for burning is in excess of temperatures of 360° F, which should not be a problem if you stay within manufacturers' recommendations. However, uneven oven heating and lack of adequate oven circulation may cause spot burning even at the lower oven settings. For this reason, polymer clay should not be left unattended in the oven.

Caution should also be taken not to ingest polymer clays. Use separate tools and utensils; don't return them to kitchen duty. If you use the clays continually, it may be wise to use latex gloves for the mixing and kneading stages, though the necessity of this has not been proven. *Children should always be supervised when using polymer clays.* Remember the safety of your pets, too, as they seem to be attracted to the smell of polymer clay. Take care to keep your supplies out of the reach of little paws and jaws.

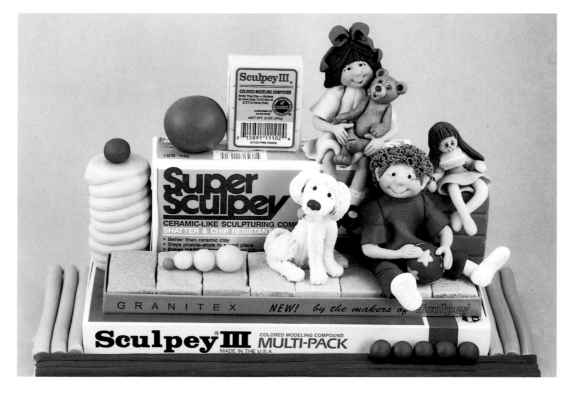

The Polyform company has a variety of clays from which to choose. The twisted pinkish clay on the left is Super Sculpey, which is primarily used for dolls and model work. The little characters were made from Sculpey III. Note that I adapted my designs to make chunkier hands and less fragile detail work.

CHAPTER TWO

Gathering Your Tools

The only tools you absolutely need to do all of the projects in this book are your oven, a baking pan, a straight-blade knife, a round toothpick, a rolling pin or brayer and a wooden dowel with a rounded end. In fact, you can even dispense with the dowel and use a sturdy brush handle, or even a pencil. After these essentials, there are many optional tools that will make the projects easier and more satisfying, but a big money expenditure is not necessary to begin.

YOUR OVEN

Your most important tool will be your oven, which may be either electric or gas. Since polymer clays are certified nontoxic when used according to manufacturers' directions, you can use your home oven for hardening (curing) the clay. Do wipe out the oven frequently after baking polymer clay, and don't cook food at the same time.

Many people find the smells of baking polymer clay to be offensive, and worry about unknown hazards, so they prefer to use a toaster oven that they have dedicated to baking polymer clay. An advantage of a toaster oven is that it can be placed in a part of your house that can be well ventilated. A disadvantage is that the oven space is small and often won't accommodate the projects in this book. It is not wise to have your polymer clay items too close to the sides and top of the oven, as there is frequently reflected heat, which can be hotter than the actual setting of the oven. When baking in a toaster oven, I have had problems with scorched tops of heads! If you must use a toaster oven, use a separate oven thermometer to test the actual temperature.

Don't bake in the microwave: These clays are plastic, with varying fillers, and are not designed for microwave use.

BAKING SURFACES

Any flat surface that will withstand temperatures of 300° F is suitable for baking polymer clay. My favorite baking surface is ceramic floor tiles in varying sizes. Other choices are metal and glass baking pans, aluminum foil and ceramic mugs. I especially like the air-bake pans that provide an insulation layer. This is important if your oven tends to burn the bottom of everything. You can create your own insulated pans by layering one pan over another.

Items baked on a shiny surface will be shiny on the bottom. To eliminate this, line the pans with kitchen parchment or baking paper, available at kitchen specialty stores. Lining the pans also keeps them safe for kitchen use. I have also used paper toweling, cardboard and cotton cloth for lining pans. Be sure and test any paper or cloth used before placing it in the oven with your masterpiece.

WORK SURFACES

I use a Formica-type tabletop as my work surface. I like the permanence of a stationary top as opposed to a temporary workboard, which may shift during use. I don't recommend wood or painted surfaces, as the clay tends to stick.

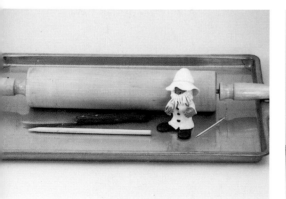

When I began making little people in 1979, these tools—plus my oven—were what I used, and they are still my basics today. The little guy is one of my early creations.

These are my favorite baking surfaces for polymer clays. Coffee mugs make great supports for propping your characters while baking.

KNIVES AND BLADES

My favorite blade is a dull, straight-edged paring knife I have used for seventeen years. It is not sharp enough to do any real cutting, but it is perfect for my sculpting work. Even the dull edge becomes a marking tool for soft wrinkles.

If I am going to cut decorative millefiori slices from a patterned polymer clay log or cane, I want an exceptionally sharp, moderately long blade. In that case, I choose a 4"-long wallpaper scraper replacement blade, available in wallpaper departments. Since the dull and sharp edges aren't clearly marked, making it easy to accidentally pick the scraper up by the blade, I usually bake a clay guard, which I superglue to the dull edge. You could also mark one side with nail polish.

A similar but sharper blade is the tissue blade, available from medical supply houses. Other useful blades are single-edged razor blades for tiny straight cuts, and craft blades, such as the OLFA or X-Acto, for carving baked clay.

NEEDLE TOOLS

A round toothpick is the best all-around pointed tool to have in your supply case. But consider adding some other needle tools for special uses. Look in your local needlecraft shop for dull, thick tapestry needles, long doll-sculpting needles and a variety of knitting needles. To make them easier to hold, make a handle from polymer clay and bake it. The handle can serve a double purpose if you make the round end the same size as eye sockets or earholes. Very useful! Commercial needle tools with wood or metal handles are also available in your local craft supply outlet.

ROLLERS

For many years I used a wood rolling pin to flatten sheets of clay. If you choose a wood rolling pin, it is essential to keep it very clean, as any clay that sticks to it will attract more clay,

These are my most frequently used blades, with each one having a specific purpose. The brown-handled one in the center is my long-time partner. We began clay work together back in the 1970s.

and you will soon have a mess. A smooth surface can be maintained by rubbing the rolling pin briskly with a soft, dry cloth. Repeat this frequently as you work. Small brayers and wallpaper seam rollers can also be useful. Brayers, found with printing supplies in art stores, and seam rollers, found in wallpaper departments, come in wood, rubber, metal and a Lucite-type material. I am partial to my Lucite one, which rarely seems to need cleaning.

If you are serious about your work with polymer clay, you will soon need a pasta machine. (I used the word *need* intentionally!) For ten years I used a rolling pin and had, quite successfully, learned to work around any problems. Only after a friend *insisted* that I try a pasta machine did I realize how much work and pain I could save myself!

If you do buy a pasta machine, be sure that you get a well-made one

Search your sewing drawer for all shapes and sizes of needles—they are terrific for clay work. The marbled handles are made from clay and then baked.

with a smooth surface roller and gears that really align. There are some cheap ones on the market that will not make you happy.

EXTRUDERS

There are a variety of extruders on the market that can be used to create strings or ropes of clay. The most common is the garlic press. The pasta machine cutting attachments can also be used for making multiple strips. The most useful, if you are using a soft clay such as Sculpey III, may be the Kemper Klay Gun, which comes with nineteen interchangeable discs.

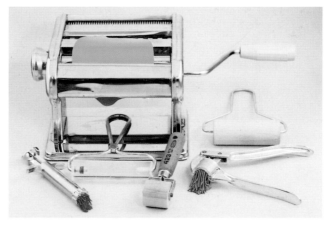

The pasta machine is now the queen of my rolling court, but each of the other rollers has its uses. I seldom use the cutting blades on the pasta machine, preferring to cut by hand. For tiny ropes I use the garlic press or Klay Gun.

A Well-Stocked Tool Chest

The rest of the chapter covers some specialized tools you might consider adding to your own easy-to-reach tool chest.

CUTTERS
While any ordinary cookie cutter can be used with polymer clays, there are special craft pattern cutters on the market that are sized for tiny replicas of common shapes. These are especially useful for adding trim to clothing and accessories. Also consider cake decorating and canapé sets.

SCULPTING TOOLS
Remember, as you search for the perfect tool, that it is not the tool that makes a terrific sculpture—it's you! With that in mind, anything that "works" can be called a sculpting tool. But there are some specialized ones on the market. Most of the commercially available ones are too large for the projects in this book, but go to a ceramic supplier and check out the variety of wood, metal and plastic shapes available. Specialized tool suppliers are listed under Resources in the back of this book.

FINGERNAIL TOOL
For fingernails, I use a special tool that my husband, Dan, custom makes from stainless steel in ten sizes. The indented ends create the perfect roundness of a tiny fingernail. You can duplicate the shape of this tool by rolling a thin clay rope the same diameter as your desired nail. Press a smooth groove into each end, then bake it. Now press this against the ends of little fingers to make fingernail impressions.

CLAYBRUSH TOOL
My favorite tools for doing final smoothing are good-quality no. 2 to no. 4 sable filbert paintbrushes. To make the bristles slightly stiff, groom a little raw clay into them, stroking in the direction of the bristles to keep them smooth. Now use this to "smooth" into tiny corners. As the bristles become clogged and stiff, clean them with waterless hand cleaner. Vary the size of the brush for the size of your sculpture. This tool is referred to as a "claybrush" in later chapters.

SURFACE TEXTURES
Press polymer clay to any rough surface and see how easily it copies the surface texture. You can use this quality to mimic the look and feel of almost anything. To make your characters' clay clothes mimic the weave of cotton, linen or lace, just press your flattened clay pieces against clean,

I gathered these tools from my worktable, where I keep them within easy reach. Experiment with objects around your home—anything that creates an interesting or useful effect can become an invaluable tool.

lint-free fabric. To make a convincing leaf, press your flattened clay leaf shape against a real leaf—a favorite of mine is the cucumber leaf. Also consider the textures and patterns of rubber stamps, leather tools and cake decorating tools. Take thirty minutes and walk around your house—or the local hardware store—taking texture prints.

PAINTS, POWDERS AND FOILS

Because the surface of polymer clay is slightly sticky, any powdery substance applied to the unbaked surface will become somewhat permanent. You'll see that I sometimes add a touch of blush for color to cheeks and knuckles. There are art powders made for this purpose, but also try chalk, makeup, pastels and common old dirt. If the baked piece will get heavy wear, protect the surface with a brush-on matte finish made especially for polymer clays.

Don't apply untested lacquers or sealers to polymer clay, as there are sometimes reactions that turn the surface sticky after a period of days—or sometimes weeks. Play it safe and use the manufacturer's recommended surface sealers.

After the piece is baked, it can be painted with acrylic paint. If the surface is very smooth, you may have some trouble with permanent adhesion. For this reason, I try to avoid paint unless it is for eyes and facial detail, or to provide a stained look on a textured surface.

STORAGE

The simplest storage containers are plastic bags. Since the polymer clays do not air dry, airtight bags are not necessary. Avoid Styrofoam-type containers and rigid plastic, as these sometimes react with the clay.

FOOD PROCESSORS

My favorite tool, next to the pasta machine, is the food processor. Believing that I should do things the "simple" way, I worked very hard for many years to mix and condition my FIMO by hand. Now, with a food processor, the chore is little more than an inconvenience. If you will be doing large quantities of clay, buy one with a 5- or 7-cup bowl. The small 2-cup size works well if you will only be conditioning two ounces at a time. Of course, like the pasta machine, the food processor is not a necessity, but. . . .

CLEANUP

To keep your hands and work surface clean and lint free, keep some waterless hand cleaner and a towel or some baby wipes on your worktable. An added benefit of the waterless hand cleaner is that it can be brushed or rubbed onto the unbaked clay surface to smooth out irregularities and fingerprints. Use this process sparingly, as it will make the surface sticky.

This has become my one indispensable piece of equipment. If you use one of the very soft clays, you probably won't need a food processor. But any of you who use stiff clays *deserve* to get one!

CHAPTER THREE

Practicing the Basic Techniques

KEEP IT CLEAN

At the risk of sounding like a nag, I'm going to caution you first about starting with clean hands. These soft and slightly sticky polymer clays pick up everything! Now check to see what you are wearing. Fuzzy sweaters and dark or new clothing could be leaving stray fibers in the air. It is the nature of polymer clay to pick up any and all lint and dust floating around innocently doing its thing.

I like to keep some waterless hand cleaner and a lint-free, well-washed cloth on my worktable to give my hands a last-minute once-over before I begin. Another handy option is disposable baby wipes.

CONDITIONING

Before the clay can be used, it must be soft and pliable. The amount of time you will need to devote to conditioning your polymer clay depends on what brand you have chosen to use. If you have one of the softer varieties such as Sculpey III or Cernit, you may find it ready to use directly from the package. If so, just twist the clay and knead it slightly to make sure that all of the clay in the package is of a uniform consistency. You won't need to rewrap the leftover clay unless you are going to leave it for a period of several days; then you might want to wrap it in order to keep it clean.

If you have one of the stiffer varieties, such as FIMO, ProMat or

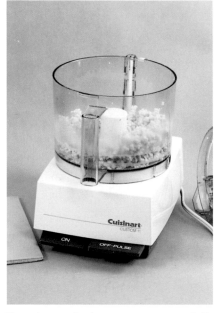

If you have a food processor you can dedicate to your polymer clay use, hurrah! Cut the clay into small chunks and process on high for approximately one minute, or until the mix just starts to clump together into bigger pieces resembling cottage cheese. Mixing clay is hard on the gears, so be watchful. Also, as the clay gets warm from the friction of the gears, it will get stickier.

Remove the clay from the bowl and knead, mix and twist until the clay is of a uniform color and consistency.

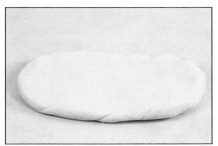

Flatten the mixture into a pancake shape to ready it for rolling. If the pancake is too thick or too cold, the clay will crack and fall apart at the edges.

Friendly Clay, you will need to warm it, then chop or break it into small pieces and knead and twist until it's smooth and elastic. Warming can be done by hand, in a pocket, by sitting on it, by placing it in a clay warmer or very low heating pad, or by placing it in a bag in hot (not boiling) water. If, after ten minutes of kneading, the

clay seems very stiff, add a softer clay or kneading compound, such as FIMO's Mix Quick or Friendly Clay Super Softener, to the mixture. Just twist and knead, twist and knead, until it returns to a uniform color. A faster option is to use a food processor.

BALLS, CONES AND ROPES

Many parts of my clay figures start with balls, cones and ropes. Sounds easy, doesn't it? But let's practice anyway. It's harder than it looks to roll a perfectly smooth ball or rope, or a uniformly round cone.

The first problem you may notice is dirty spots. If you keep getting dirty spots, clean your hands again, even if it's the fifth time.

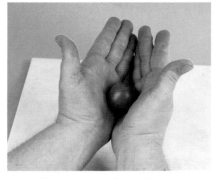

I start all my shapes with a ball, as that form allows for easy smoothing of the surface.

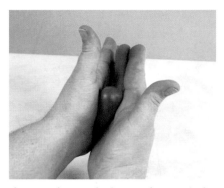

The next shape, which I use frequently for hats, armatures, sleeves and pant legs is the cone. To make this, roll a smooth ball, then place your hands in a *V* shape and roll the ball back and forth in a sliding motion.

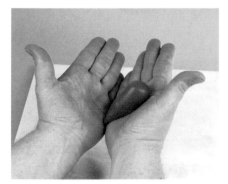

Most of the pressure should be on the bottom part of your palms, so that the ball stays rounded at the top and becomes pointed at the bottom.

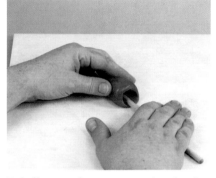

To hollow out the cone, use a dowel rod or blunt paintbrush handle. Lay the cone on its side, holding it firmly so it doesn't roll, insert the handle and, with a flat hand, roll back and forth like a miniature rolling pin.

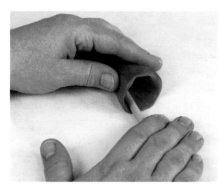

Now turn the cone and roll another spot. Continue until the cone is the desired size.

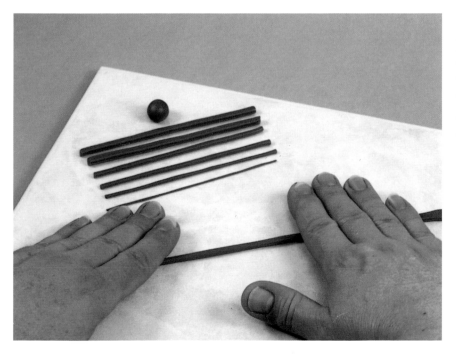

Next, try making a thin, uniform rope. Beginners usually press too hard, which makes an uneven rope. The trick is to use light, uniform pressure as you move your hands steadily farther and farther apart. This stretches the clay and keeps a uniform surface tension. Rope shapes are used for arms, legs, hair and clothing trim.

ROLLING SHEETS

My designs also call for frequent use of flat sheets of clay. Although I now groan at having to do without my pasta machine, for years I got excellent results when rolling by hand. If you don't do enough clay work to justify the expense of dedicating a pasta machine just for clay use, simply be extra careful to have a clean, dry and stationary work surface for rolling.

Some artists choose to roll the clay pancake between sheets of waxed paper. I have found that this is cumbersome, as the waxed paper sometimes wrinkles.

DRAPING AND LAYERING

My techniques depend heavily on draping or layering sheets of clay to make them simulate clothing pieces. I sewed before I ever worked with clay, and you can see that influence in my clay work. One big advantage of clay is that it stretches, so it is much easier to get an adequate fit with clay than with fabric.

Being sure that the surface of the clay is smooth and bubble free is necessary before you begin to drape. I pat the sheets between my hands to remove bubbles. If that doesn't work, try slicing the bubbles with a sharp razor blade. You can also camouflage

To roll clay sheets with a pasta machine, start with a flat pancake, as shown on page eighteen. Stretch the pancake to the width of the machine's opening, then roll it through on the thickest setting. Repeat at progressively thinner settings. When using the pasta machine to mix clay, always run the pancake through with the fold at the side or bottom to prevent formation of air bubbles.

any irregularities—plus add an interesting surface—by pressing a textured fabric or embossing sheet onto the surface. If you place a sheet of fabric under the clay while you are pressing it, you will eliminate aggravating sticking and tearing.

Graceful draping is dependent on just the right consistency of clay. If it is too cold and stiff, it will crack when you try to fold it. If it is too soft, it will stretch and droop. If you are careful, you can create gathers or pleats without fingerprints or cracked areas. If you have trouble with cracks, try

To create flat sheets with a rolling pin or brayer, first form the clay into a smooth, round ball. Be certain that your work surface is very dry and clean. Flatten the ball between your hands into a thin pancake shape. Now press one edge slightly to anchor it to the work surface. Roll the clay three or four times, rolling in one direction only. Then lift the clay, flip it, anchor it again and roll in another direction. Repeat until the clay is the desired thickness. If the clay sticks to the board or the rolling pin, rub the surfaces briskly with a soft cloth to remove any traces of clay. Also, pat smooth any roughened areas of the clay pancake, as these will tend to be sticky.

mixing your clay again with more softener added. If your clay stretches and refuses to hold its shape while you are working, you either rolled it too thin or are using a clay that is too soft. Try rolling thicker sheets.

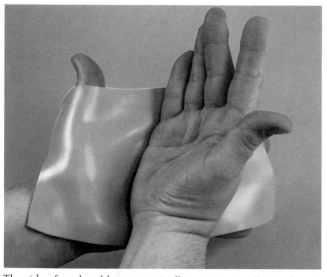

The side of my hand becomes a "rolling pin" as I roll it back and forth across the surface of this sheet to remove irregularities.

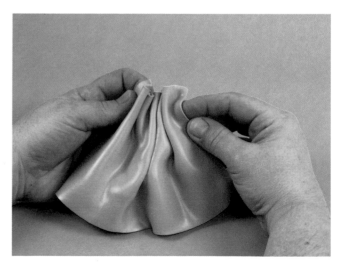

Using a freshly rolled sheet of clay that is still slightly warm, try folding it into soft gathers like those at the top of a skirt. Hold it gently to avoid flattening the gathers.

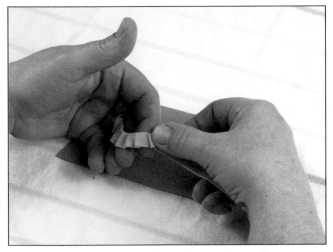

Practice pressing in tiny accordion pleats with your fingers.

Use soft tools, such as a brush, to position trims and folds. This will eliminate fingerprints and tool marks.

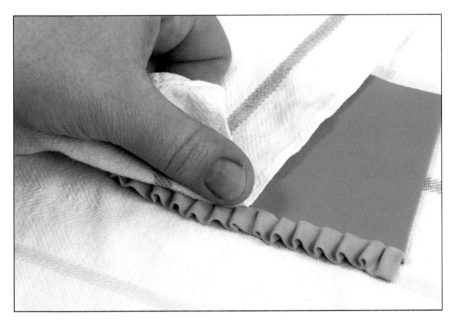

Pressing with a cloth will camouflage fingerprints and help folds be less bulky. Notice that I placed my clay on top of the fabric to prevent it from sticking to the table.

BAKING

Even if you do everything else right with your polymer clay, your piece can be ruined if you underbake it or bake it at too high a temperature. Whichever oven you choose to use (see chapter two, page 14), the most important consideration is an accurate temperature reading. All polymer clay brands are hardened permanently by baking at temperatures between 215° F and 275° F. Baking times vary depending on the thickness of the piece, but most directions specify twenty to thirty minutes. Always read the directions on your package of clay before baking.

Items that are underbaked—either in time, temperature or both—are very fragile. Some artists decrease the temperature in order to reduce the darkening that comes with higher temperatures, but I would rather adjust for the darkening by mixing lighter colors of clay. These characters are too much work (and too wonderful!) to risk having them easily broken due to inadequate curing, so I rarely bake under 250° F—and never less than a half hour, unless I am doing multiple bakings on one piece.

An exception is when I am using plastic eyes in my dolls: Then I lower the temperature to 235°–250° F to reduce the risk of melting the eyes. For added durability, some artists extend the length of the baking time. In general this appears to be safe, as long as one doesn't go over the recommended temperature. Sculpey III should never be overbaked, as it scorches very easily.

Always keep an eye on the oven: Oven irregularity or human error can cause an actual fire. I advise testing your oven with a separate oven thermometer if you are at all in doubt of your oven's performance. All pieces in this book are baked in a preheated oven at 265° F for thirty minutes. For the final bake, the oven is turned off while the piece cools.

CHAPTER FOUR

Making Basic Body Parts

Creating little hands, feet and faces seems to be impossibly hard at first. But it isn't. If you can follow a recipe for making rolled Christmas cookies, or if you can put together a kid's toy stroller, you can follow the steps for making hands, feet and faces. I have taught hundreds of people how to do this—so I know you can do it, too.

As you practice these steps, you are apt to find ways to do them that make more sense to you. If you do, then by all means change the steps. When I began, I couldn't find anyone to teach me, so I learned by trial and error. Then, as I began teaching, and sometimes taking classes, I gradually learned to "see the forms" more clearly. I'm still learning. The same is bound to happen to you. The learning and seeing that happen inside your head are often more important to the end result than how you are manipulating your fingers and tools.

> **TIP**
>
> If you are using polymer clay for the first time, start with a stiff clay like FIMO or Friendly Clay. These firmer clays will be more forgiving of unsure motions, and will fingerprint less easily. As your skills and "touch" become more controlled, try the softer clays.

Making Hands

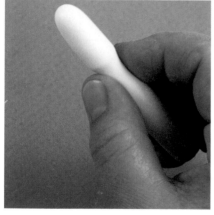

Roll a smooth ball, then a tube shape that is as thick as the arm of your character. (Do each step for both arms so that they will match, even though I will only be showing you one arm in the pictures.) Determine how long the hand will be, then roll the wrist between your fingers. It is better to have the wrist too thick at this stage than too thin.

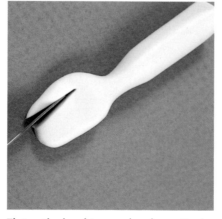

Flatten the hand in a wedge shape. Don't press too hard! You don't want it to look smashed. Cut a line for the thumb. Note that the hand narrows at the finger end.

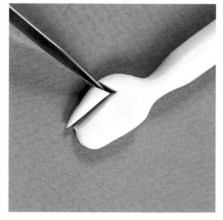

Trim the length of the thumb. It will look very short, but usually this area of the clay is thick, so, as you smooth the cut edges in the next step, the thumb will lengthen.

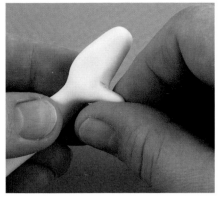

Smooth the cut edges between your fingers. Stretch the thumb so that the hand resembles a mitten. See how your own thumb is rooted at the base of your hand and not up by your fingers? Is the thumb in the right place?

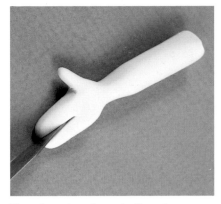

Place the point of your knife at the center point of your hand and just slightly toward the little-finger side. Cut straight down to make the center line between the ring and middle fingers.

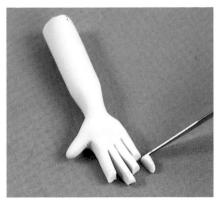

Now cut once on each side to make four fingers. Trim the ends of the fingers to adjust the lengths, using your own hand as a guide. Is the thumb still at the base of the hand? If not, move it down.

Smooth and round the cut ends of each finger. If the clay is warm and well conditioned, you should be able to bend the other fingers out of the way while you smooth one. Don't worry about the inside edges of the fingers. This is a beginning hand!

Use the fingernail tool, which has a slight groove at the end, to press in the nails. You can make this shape from clay and then bake it to make your own custom-made tool. For a flatter fingernail, use the head of a small carpenter tack or nail. Notice that your thumb is turned slightly so that your thumbnail is not in the same plane as the fingernails.

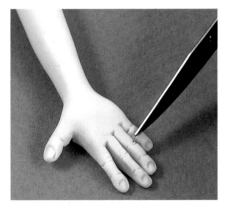

Use your knife or a thin needle tool to mark in the knuckle lines. I usually roll the knife around the edge slightly to make a curved line.

On the palm side, use a brush handle to roll an indentation at the bottom of the palm.

Look at your own hand. See the hollow in the middle of your palm? To simulate this, roll the brush handle from just above the thumb to the bottom center of the hand.

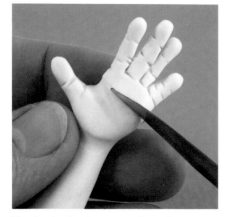

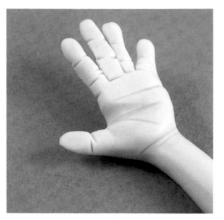

Use the knife edge or needle tool to press in the lines of the palm. Avoid scratching the surface with the needle tool, as this leaves little clay crumbs. Pressing and rolling seem to work better for me.

Try to copy all the lines and curves of your own hand. Don't forget to press wrinkles where the wrist bends.

At this point the hand is very flat. Stop for a minute and look at your own hand. Move your thumb to touch your little finger. See how the whole side of your hand moves along with your thumb? Now go back to your clay hand and press the thumb and the base of the thumb around to the side of the hand. Ouch! Almost hurt, didn't it?

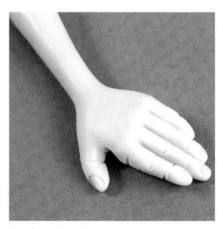

To make knuckles, smudge the clay toward the knuckles: first from the fingers toward the knuckles, then from the back of the hand toward the knuckles. Do this in a gentle lifting motion. Now use the claybrush tool to smooth between the fingers and knuckles.

Now, what shall we do about that cellulite on the arm? I roll the wrist and arm between the flat spots at the base of my palm, near the thumb. Try it.

Ah, the finished hand. For a younger-looking hand, don't make the wrinkles or knuckles so pronounced, and keep the fingers shorter.

Making Feet

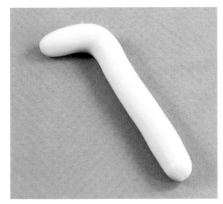

Roll a tube shape as thick as the calf of your character. Determine how long the foot will be, then turn the ankle at this point—but don't flatten it.

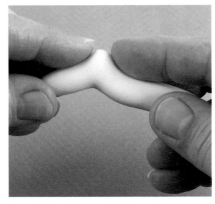

Press the heel into a ball shape that extends beyond the leg. Notice that I am not touching the top of the foot. I sometimes accidentally squash the foot so I've learned not to hold it there.

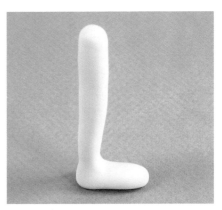

Check that the foot sits flat on the table, with a little outward bulge for the heel. If there isn't a dip just above the heel, roll the brush handle across this area. Now smooth and trim it if it's too long.

Gently press the foot to make it taper toward the toe. Trim at an angle, making the big toe the longest. Cut four lines to make toes. Cut ends to adjust lengths.

Smooth the cut ends of each toe. Create toenails the same way you created fingernails. Use a blunt blade to press in the lines on the sides of the toes and at the joints.

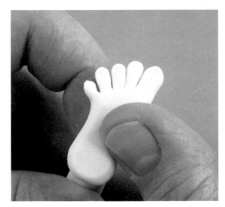

On the bottom side, use your finger to roll an indentation across the big-toe side of the foot. This will create an arch.

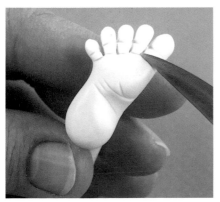

Use the knife edge or needle tool to press in the lines on the foot bottom. Avoid scratching the surface with the needle tool, as it makes it look rough.

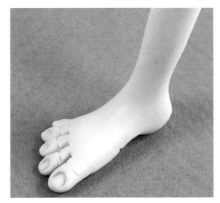

Align the toes and position the foot.

Making Simple Faces

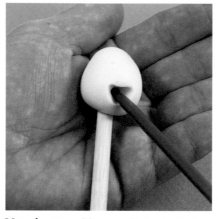

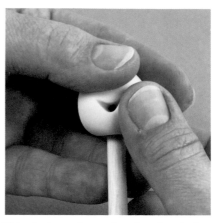

Head. Begin with a ball. Roll the ball into one of two basic shapes: either an egg with the small end down or an egg with the large end down. Place the head on a stick or brush handle to make it easier to hold, being careful not to poke the stick too far into the ball.

Mouth. Use a blunt needle tool to indent a deep, smooth mouth shape. The size of the needle you use depends on the size of the head. Too thin a needle or too shallow a hole makes a pinched-looking mouth. Make the mouth bigger than you want it as you will close it in the next step.

This closing action makes the edges look softer and more rounded—not so tool-made. Gently press the corners of the mouth toward each other. If you press too hard you will leave a giant finger mark. Don't do that!

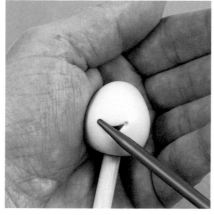

Add a dimple on either side by pressing a blunt tool against the corners of the mouth. Notice that the tool is nearly parallel to the mouth.

Soften the marks with the claybrush tool. Make the indentation look gradual.

Roll your thumb just above the mouth to create a cheek line.

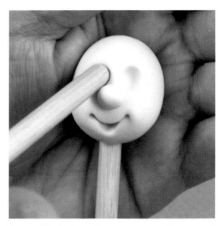

Nose. Start the nose with a tiny ball, and roll it into a teardrop shape. Set the nose just below the middle of the face. (Whoa, this is a huge nose, isn't it? But being able to overemphasize features is what makes caricatures fun. Experiment with different sizes and shapes to vary the effect—and the personality.)

Use your finger or a blunt tool to blend the top of the nose into the face. On these simple characters I don't spend a lot of time blending the underside of the nose and giving it detail. That comes in chapter six.

Eyes. To indent the eye area, roll a round tool on each side of the nose. If you don't have the right size round tool, make one from clay and bake it.

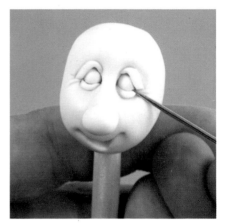

Eyeballs. Bake a selection of different sizes of tiny white clay balls to use for eyeballs. Use the round clay tool to press prebaked eyeballs in place. On caricatures, you can make the eyes any size—from small and beady to exaggeratedly huge. Use the claybrush tool to soften lines and forms.

Eyelids. Roll four tiny comma-shaped pieces for eyelids—two larger and two smaller. Pick these up with the needle tool and place a larger one over and a smaller one under each eye. Position with a brush to prevent gouges.

Use a needle tool to indent the corners of the eyes and to roll in wrinkles.

Adding Details

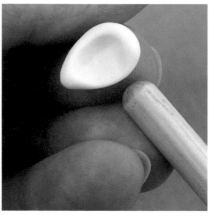

Nostrils. Use a sharp needle tool to make tiny nostrils. Be sure to indent them right on the line where the nose meets the face: Placing them higher will give your character a pig snout. At this point, check out the shape of the face. Has it distorted? My faces tend to get too fat, so I put them on a diet by pressing them between my palms. If the chin is too fleshy, smudge some of the clay away from the face, toward the back and sides of the head.

Ears. Simple ears start with a ball, which is then rolled into a teardrop shape. Flatten the teardrop slightly. Use a round tool to hollow out one side of the ear.

Place the ear onto the side of the head. Press in place with the round tool. Roll and smooth the joint line with a blunt needle tool and a brush. Use a smaller round tool to make a hole in the ear. Pull the ear forward and shape sides.

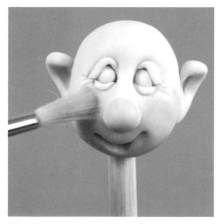

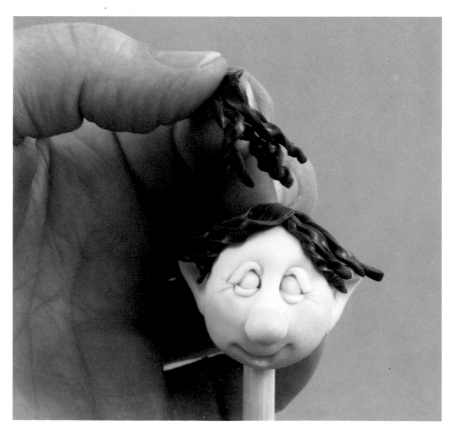

Cheeks. Brush a matte makeup blush or powdered pink chalk on the cheeks and nose. Avoid blushes and chalks that leave a metallic shine.

Hair. Add hair, if desired. I usually wait to add hair until after the head is on the body, but this little guy was crying out for hair for the sake of the picture, so I'll add some now. Chapter five covers methods for creating several different hair types and colors.

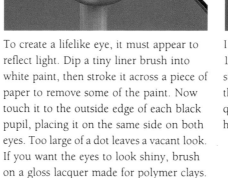

Painting the Eyes. The eyes are painted after the character is baked. Look in the mirror and note that your entire iris (the colored part) only shows when you open your eyes very wide. Normally it is partially covered by your eyelids. Determine how large you want the iris to be. Use acrylic paint and a no. 1 brush to paint in the iris: Be sure not to load the brush too heavily with paint. Let it dry. Now load the tip of the brush with black paint. Touch it lightly to what appears to be the center of the circular iris.

To create a lifelike eye, it must appear to reflect light. Dip a tiny liner brush into white paint, then stroke it across a piece of paper to remove some of the paint. Now touch it to the outside edge of each black pupil, placing it on the same side on both eyes. Too large of a dot leaves a vacant look. If you want the eyes to look shiny, brush on a gloss lacquer made for polymer clays.

I make eyebrows and eyelashes with a no. 1 liner brush. Dip it into brown paint, then stroke across a sheet of scrap paper until the bristles are nearly dry. Now, with a quick upward stroke, lightly paint in one hair at a time.

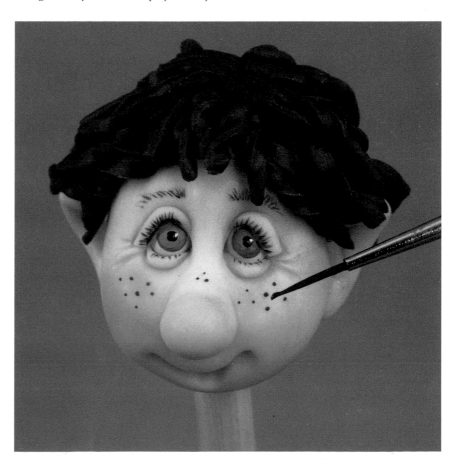

To create freckles, use a liner brush to lightly dot on tiny brown spots. If you want indistinct spots, tap cheeks lightly and repeatedly with your dry finger while the dots are still wet.

CHAPTER FIVE

The Neighborhood Kids: Starting Simple

Yes, you too can create these little people. Just begin with the first step for character number one and before you know it you will see there, sitting in front of you, an almost-alive little being. The projects in this chapter are set up in a series of lessons—each character builds on the steps learned in the previous lesson. You can begin with any of the Neighborhood Kids, but it will be easiest for you if you begin with Sweet Suzette.

If you are like the majority of people out there, you have turned to this part of the book without reading the first four chapters. (I do the same thing!) Don't worry. All basic directions are given in this chapter, so you *can* begin right here. But if you get stuck or are dissatisfied with what you have made, turn to the previous chapters or the Problems and Solutions section at the back of this book. Don't feel that you have to copy my characters *exactly*. Even I can't make exact duplicates of a character that I've made before. Having unrealistic expectations for yourself is the quickest way to kill the joy of a project. So, be easy on yourself—make your character a close friend or relative of my original.

READYING THE CLAY

The project colors for this chapter were chosen with economy in mind. Starting with just twelve colors of clay, you can mix all of the variations needed for the Neighborhood Kids. The exact color mixes will be given in each project. Start by warming each color, then kneading and twisting until the clay is of uniform consistency and color. If the clay seems too stiff, add a kneading medium, such as Mix Quick, until the clay is the desired consistency. I added approximately one part Mix Quick to every four parts FIMO used for the models.

ROLLING SHEETS OF CLAY

If you are using one of the stiffer polymer clays, roll the sheets to approximately $1/16''$ thick. Make the sheets slightly thicker if the figure will be handled a lot or if you are using one of the softer (or weaker) clays.

BAKING

All characters in this chapter are baked in stages to make them easier to handle. Before starting, read the directions so that you can plan for that "waiting" time by mixing clay or prepping the next steps. Read the package for the manufacturer's baking recommendations. Usually I bake at the highest and longest recommended temperature and time. After the final bake, the character is cooled in the oven to allow for a little extra bake time. The characters are very fragile while hot, so be careful about shifting their positions.

WHAT YOU'LL NEED FOR THESE PROJECTS:
- Polymer clay:
  - pink and caramel flesh colors
  - black
  - blue
  - golden yellow
  - light turquoise
  - magenta
  - ochre
  - transparent
  - turquoise green
  - violet
  - white
- Kneading medium, such as Mix Quick
- A selection of prebaked white-clay eyeballs $1/8''$ to $3/16''$ in diameter
- FIMO gloss lacquer
- Acrylic paint (in tube or jar):
  - brown
  - black
  - white
  - blue
- Pink makeup blush
- Round toothpicks
- Block of wood or other oven-safe square-edged form
- Knife
- Rolling pin or brayer
- Pasta machine (optional)
- Assorted brushes (no. 2 or no. 3 filbert, no. 3 round, no. 1 liner)
- Oven
- Oven thermometer
- Needle tools (both sharp and blunt)
- Ruler
- Fabric for texture
- Sturdy brush handle or 7"-long piece of $1/4''$ dowel
- Rubber stamp (for Stan only)
- Baby powder (for Stan only)

Sweet Suzette

Sweet Suzette is never loud and seldom gets into trouble on the playground, and she *never* misses a thing. Her biggest wish is to become brave enough to climb to the top of the jungle gym. She doesn't know it yet, but someday she will head her own Fortune 500 company.

STEP 1   MIXING COLORS

Suzette's hair is five parts transparent mixed with one part ochre. Her dress is a mix of equal parts of white and violet. The pale pink is seven parts white mixed with one part magenta. You will also need flesh pink, black and white.

STEP 2   UNDERWEAR

Yes, underwear does come first, even for little clay people. Roll a 1¼"-diameter ball of white clay into a 2½"-tall cone. Insert a dowel or sturdy brush handle halfway into the cone. Hold the cone steady with one hand while rolling the dowel back and forth, like a miniature rolling pin, with the other hand. This will flatten just one side of the cone; keep repositioning the cone so that all sides are thinned.

Insert your thumb into the cone and bend it in half, keeping skirt area open. Set the cone on an oven-safe wooden bench or block of wood. Insert a toothpick spine.

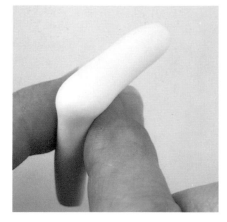

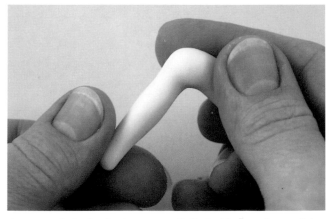

STEP 3   LEGS

Roll two ¾"-diameter balls of flesh clay. Roll each into a smooth tube 2½" long. Bend tube softly in half. To form knee and calf, use your two pointer fingers and grasp the leg just below the knee and roll gently. Repeat above the knee.

Now smooth the leg (and remove cellulite) with a gentle smudging and stretching motion. Taper the ankle.

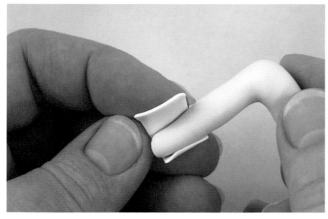

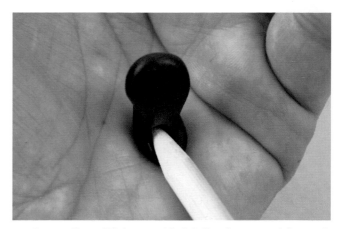

STEP 4 SHOES AND SOCKS

For socks, cut two pieces approximately ½″ × ¾″ from flattened white clay. Wrap pieces around ankle. Trim back seam of sock so that the edges do not overlap. Roll ankle between fingers to smooth.

For shoes, roll two ⅝″-diameter black balls. Shape top of shoe with your fingers. Use brush handle to hollow out space for ankle.

Press ankle in place, then shape shoe again. From white clay, roll two ³⁄₁₆″-diameter balls. Flatten them between your fingers, then press one over the top of each shoe, just slightly below the seam where shoe and ankle meet. For the strap, flatten a tiny black rope, approximately ³⁄₈″ × ⅛″, and press over the seam where Suzette's ankle and shoe meet. Use knife point to cut in buttonhole. For button, press a tiny black ball to bottom of buttonhole.

> **TIP**
>
> To save time on future projects, roll out an assortment of tiny white balls and bake them along with Suzette; each project in this book will call for prebaked eyeballs, and having different sizes on hand will allow you to choose the pair that looks best with each character's expression.

STEP 5 THE FIRST BAKE

Position legs into underwear. Press underskirt firmly around legs. Bake Sweet Suzette in a preheated 265° F oven for thirty minutes. It is tempting to forget this baking step, as having to stop breaks up the creative flow. You can skip it and just keep going, but working with a hardened inner armature makes it *much* easier—plus there is less of a tendency for her chin to gradually sink into her chest as you work intently on her hair, which just won't do for a pretty little thing like Suzette.

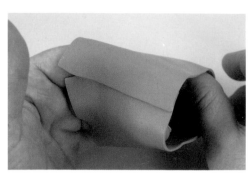

STEP 6   DRESS

From a sheet of light-violet, cut a 2½″ × 7½″ rectangle. Create texture by pressing between fabric pieces. Overlap short ends of dress to create a tube.

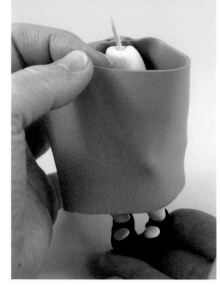

Slip dress over Suzette's body. (Don't worry about messing up her hair—it's still on the table!)

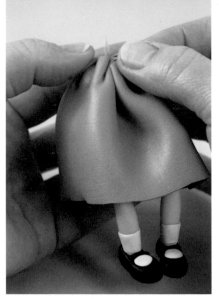

Gather dress around neck. Press in place, being careful not to leave any fingerprints where they will show below the collar. One way to press without fingerprints is to lay the texturing cloth over the gathers, and then pat them into place. Stretch the back of the skirt to cover her underwear.

Use a soft brush to lift folds and reposition them.

STEP 7   SLEEVES

From light violet, roll two ⅝″-diameter balls. Hollow each with brush handle. Roll on fabric for texture.

Press sleeves in place, using handle to position them. Note the position of my hand in the picture. I try not to touch the dress, as the gathers are easy to flatten.

STEP 8   COLLAR

From flattened light-pink clay, cut a 1″ circle. Use a ⅜″ punch cutter or a knife to remove center of circle. Press with fabric for texture.

Cut a narrow wedge out of one side of collar. From flattened white, cut a strip 3″ × ¼″. Use the sharp needle tool to impress a scalloped edge, indenting every ³⁄₁₆″, into the white trim. Use sharp and blunt needle tools to create a pattern of dots around the collar. Be creative: It doesn't have to be exactly like mine.

Roll a short ⅜″-thick tube for the neck and press it in place over toothpick. Position collar. Don't make it too tight—she is a little kid, you know, and likes to run and play.

Use your fingers to smoothly close the corners of her mouth. Be gentle, as a firm push will cause her to look bedraggled. Lots of small smudging motions are most effective. If she has too much chin area, smudge it smoothly under her chin and toward the back of her head. (Hmmmm, I wish it were that easy on my own chin!) For her nose, roll a tiny ⅛" ball of flesh. Press it just below the middle line of her face. Using a blunt needle tool, blend the top edge into her face. Use a soft brush stiffened slightly with unbaked clay (claybrush tool) to smooth the sides of her nose. Since she has such a tiny nose, omit nostrils.

STEP 9   FACE

From light-pink flesh clay, roll a 1" ball. Use a blunt needle tool to push in a hole for the mouth. Roll the tool *smoothly* up at each corner of the mouth.

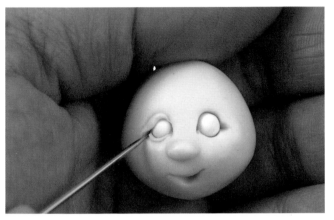

STEP 10   EYES

Indent a circle for each eye with a rounded tool. Press prebaked white-clay eyeballs into place. Look at her from each side and from an upsidedown position (her, not you!) to see that the eyes are equally spaced. Use a sharp needle tool to indent each corner of her eyes. Roll four tiny commas for eyelids. Position the smaller ones below each eye, lifting them into place with the sharp needle tool. Position the larger ones above each eye, flattening them slightly. Place the head onto her neck.

STEP 11   HANDS

Using a tube approximately 2" × ¼", make hands following directions on pages 22-24. Suzette's hands are ½" long from fingertip to wrist. Bend elbow ¾" from wrist. Insert arms into sleeves. Press top of sleeves with texturing cloth to make sure arms are firmly attached to the sleeves. Lightly brush some color (makeup blush or powdered chalk) onto her cheeks and knuckles.

STEP 12   HAIR

From a sheet of transparent and ochre mix, cut a 5" × 2" rectangle. Cut into short sections and fringe with knife.

Twist hair strands with your fingers.

"Style" hair as you press short sections in place. To make a neat part, bend the last few pieces around the needle tool to camouflage the cut ends, then press in place. Roll needle to release strands.

STEP 13 BOWS

From a sheet of flattened light pink, cut a strip 3⁄16″ × 3″. Lift five strands at one side of her head and wrap a short pink piece around this ponytail. Repeat on the other side.

For the bows, cut four 5⁄8″-long pieces from the strip. Using the needle tool, pick up the end of one piece. Curve the other end toward the needle tool to form a loop. Press the loop onto the pink band. Repeat with the opposite side. Press a short piece over the center of the bow.

STEP 14 THE SECOND BAKE

Set Suzette, still on her bench, into a pre-heated oven. (Turn on the light if she's afraid of the dark.) Bake for thirty minutes. Let her cool in the oven.

STEP 15 PAINTING EYES

When cool, paint Suzette's eyes with acrylic paint. Avoid using paint that's too watery, as it may not adhere to the polymer clay. Use a nearly dry no. 1 liner brush for all eyelash and eyebrow lines. Brush on eyelashes with light, upward strokes. Repeat with shorter strokes for the eyebrows. For glossy eyes, brush on a light coat of FIMO lacquer. Be careful not to let it run, or Suzette will look like she is about to cry.

1 Paint iris blue.

2 Dot brush, loaded with black paint, to the center of each eye.

3 For highlight, lightly touch white paint to the bottom right of each pupil.

Patterns

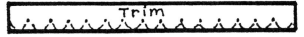

Pattern for Suzette's collar.

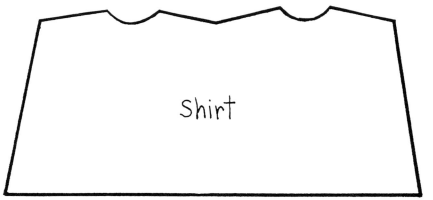

Pattern for Stan's shirt.

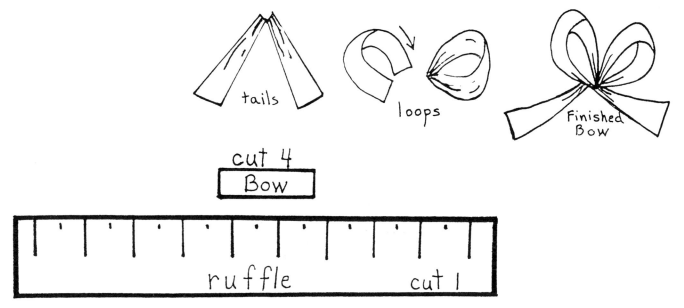

Pattern for Marissa's ruffle and bow. To pleat the ruffle, fold on the solid line, then bring to dot. Fold two bow pieces into loops and position as shown.

Studious Stan

Studious Stan is shy and easily startled. Because he's never sure what to say, he always carries a book so that he can pretend to be busy. I'll bet that you, like me, will find yourself patting him on the head and telling him that all will be OK.

Although his clothing is a bit more involved than Suzette's, with just a little round circle for a mouth and his simple sitting position, you might find him the easiest of the seven kids to make.

If you wish an even simpler project, eliminate his book.

STEP 1   MIXING COLORS

Stan's shirt is a mix of three parts white with one part yellow. For his hair, mix two parts transparent with one part caramel. The book cover is seven parts turquoise green with one part white. You will also need to condition white for underwear, the book pages and shoes, blue for pants and pink flesh for skin.

STEP 2   THE BOOK

Props are easy and fun to make from polymer clay, but they do take some advance thought. Stan's book is prebaked so that the cover will stay believably flat—like that of a real hard-covered book. To begin, cut a 2″ × 1⅜″ rectangle from flattened turquoise green. Cut a slightly smaller one from white and lay it on top of the larger one. If you want a thicker book, add more white layers.

To keep the rubber stamp from sticking to the clay, brush the surface of the book with a thin film of baby powder. Imprint pages with the rubber-stamp image of your choice. Use a dull straightedge to press in the center of the book.

Use the dull straightedge to indent the back of the book. Use a sharp knife to imprint page lines along the edges of the white squares.

To bake the book, lay it on a folded piece of firm white paper (such as a recipe card). Support the sides of the card. Bake for twenty minutes. Cool in the oven before removing.

Create more distinct images on the book by painting the pages with a coat of brown or black acrylic paint. Immediately wipe off excess. For more distinct lines, let paint dry, then sand surface with 400- and 600-grain wet-dry sandpaper. This will leave dark lines only in the recessed areas.

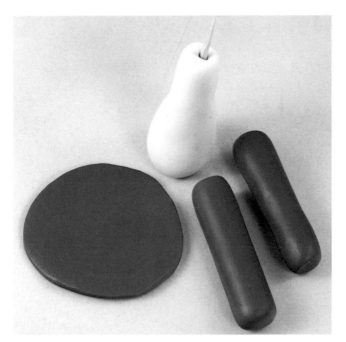

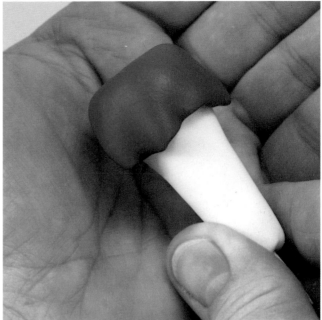

STEP 3   UNDERWEAR AND PANTS

To make the figure easier to pick up as you are working with it, you will need to make the underwear first and bake it. This will also give support to Stan's "character" as you are dressing him. From white clay, roll a 1"-diameter ball. With your hands in a V position, roll the ball into a cone 2" tall. Insert a toothpick into the small end of the cone until only ½" protrudes. Bake for twenty minutes. Cool.

From blue clay roll a ¾"-diameter ball. Flatten between your hands into a 2"-diameter pancake shape. For legs, roll two ½"-diameter logs, each 2" long.

STEP 4   FITTING THE PANTS

Press the blue pancake firmly over the bottom of the cooled underwear.

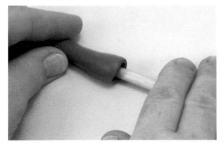

Use a sturdy handle or dowel to hollow each pant leg to the knee. At knee, push handle up slightly to form a small bulge for the kneecap.

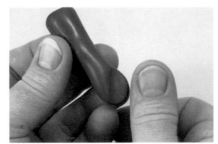

Press your thumb against the inside top of the leg to flatten it slightly.

Press legs to body, with the body sitting over the flattened area of the pant legs. Blend the edges.

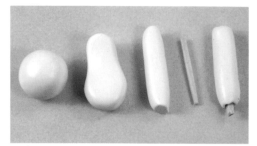

STEP 5 SHOES AND SOCKS

For each of Stan's brand new white tennis shoes, roll a ⅝"-diameter ball. Use your fingers to press the ball into the shape of a shoe. For each sock, roll a 1¼" × ⅜" rope. To be sure that his ankles don't get wobbly, insert a 1½" piece of toothpick into each sock.

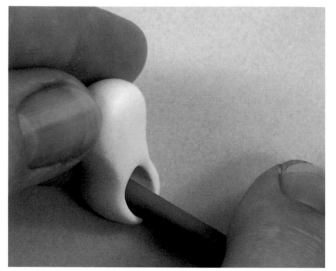

Use a brush handle to hollow a space in the shoe for placing Stan's sock.

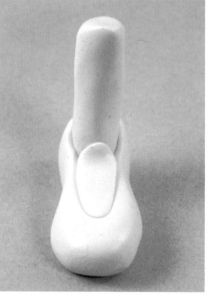

Press sock into shoe. For the shoe tongue, roll a 3/16"-diameter white ball into a ⅝"-long teardrop shape. Flatten it and press over top of shoe.

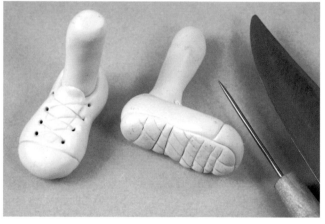

To simulate shoestrings, use needle tool to press lacing holes into tops of shoes. Use a knife to press in imitation laces. Mark in stitch lines and the tread of the shoe bottom.

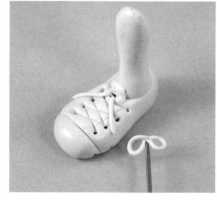

For shoestring tie, roll a long, skinny string of white clay. Keep it uniform by stretching it slightly as you roll. Cut it into eight ½"-long segments. Press two straight pieces to the top of each shoe for the tails. Form the other four pieces into loops. Lift each with the needle tool and press to shoe.

STEP 6 THE SECOND BAKE

Place Stan's body onto a baking pan. Prop his shoes with a piece of foil or kitchen parchment paper to keep them from falling flat as they bake. Bake for twenty minutes. Cool.

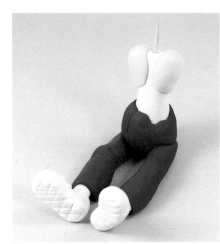

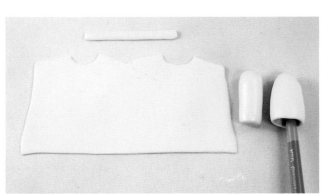

From a flattened sheet of yellow, cut Stan's shirt, using the pattern on page 37. Cut a ³⁄₁₆″ × 1³⁄₄″ piece for the neck trim. Press shirt with fabric for texture. Use a knife to cut ribbed lines into the neck trim. For each sleeve, roll a ³⁄₈″ × 1¹⁄₄″ rope. Hollow sleeves with a dowel or brush handle.

STEP 7 SHIRT AND ARMS

To pad shoulders, roll two ³⁄₈″-diameter balls. Smooth into place at the top of the cone.

◄ Form shirt into a tube shape by overlapping short ends. Press seam with fabric to get a smooth seam. (I'm sure that Stan doesn't care, but his mother is a good seamstress.)

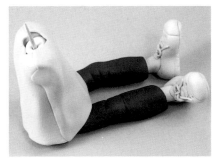

Fit shirt to body by overlapping front shoulder piece over back shoulder piece.

Press sleeves in place with the dowel; pushing too hard with your fingers may flatten the sleeves.

◄ Make arms following directions in chapter three. The arms, including the hands, begin with a 2″ × ³⁄₈″ rope; his hand is ¹⁄₂″ from fingertip to wrist. Press sleeves with fabric to make shoulders smooth. Use a needle tool or dull edge to press in wrinkle lines.

► For Stan's neck, press a ¹⁄₂″ × ³⁄₈″ rope onto the end of the toothpick. Position neck trim, overlapping in the back. Place the prebaked book into his hands

STEP 8   HEAD

Begin with a very smooth 1″-diameter ball. Roll into an egg shape. Use a blunt needle tool to press in a round mouth.

For his nose, form a ³⁄₁₆″-diameter ball into a round teardrop shape. Blend top of nose into face.

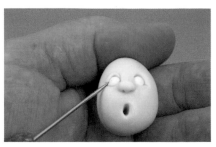

Choose two matching white, prebaked eyeballs. Press in place. For eyelids, roll four tiny comma shapes. Lift each with a needle tool and drop in place. Brush into position with your claybrush tool.

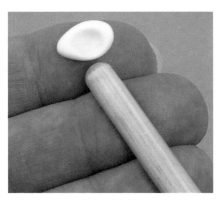

For each ear, roll a ¼″ ball. Flatten into a teardrop shape. Press center with round tool.

Press ear into place with a round tool. Press and pull the bottom of the ear to curl it forward.

STEP 9   HAIR

From flattened light caramel clay, cut a 1″ wide strip. Use a knife to fringe it, then separate pieces slightly.

Arrange hair by pressing three or four pieces at a time to his head. Add the last pieces with the needle tool. Try to simulate the look of a part.

Paint Stan's eyes, following the directions for Sweet Suzette on page 36.

STEP 10
THE THIRD BAKE

You're almost done! To add color to Stan's face, brush with makeup blush or chalk. Bake him, then let him cool in the oven. Since Stan is kind of timid, some gentle music may make the time pass more easily for him—and you!

Tomboy Tess

Tomboy Tess is always in the middle of any activity on the playground. Her bright smile and expectant eyes can cheer up even the grouchiest neighbor who happens to settle onto one of the rusting old park benches that surround the playground. Laces and frills are not her thing, because being free to tumble and play is what brings her the greatest happiness. Tess's form is a variation of Studious Stan's; if you liked making him, you should enjoy getting acquainted with Tess.

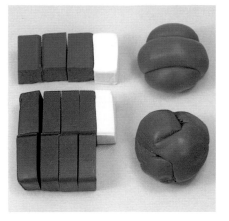

STEP 2 FROM UNDERWEAR TO THE FIRST BAKE

To make underwear, roll a 1″ ball of junk clay into a cone shape. Lay it down and turn up the smaller end— this simulates the curve of the spine. (Ask someone in the house to model this position for you so that you can visualize how the lying-down body is positioned.) Insert half a toothpick into the small end of the underwear. Press a needle tool against the larger end to form "cheeks." I suggest prebaking Tess's underwear so that it is easier to control the shape of her pants. Sometimes I skip this first prebaking step if I'm in a hurry, but if the underwear is unbaked, it's hard to retain her bottom shape when blending the legs into the pants. Bake for 20 minutes. Cool.

While the underwear is baking, roll a ⅞″ diameter ball from violet clay. Flatten it between your hands into a 2″-diameter pancake shape. For legs, roll two ½″-diameter logs, each 2″ long. Hollow legs to the knees.

STEP 1 MIXING COLORS

Tess's shirt is a mix of three parts magenta with one part white. To make up for the darkening that tends to occur during baking, I mixed one part white to the eight parts violet for her pants. To mix the shoe color, twist together a ½″ ball of white and some of the leftover shirt color. You will also need: a 1″ ball of junk, or leftover clay for underwear; black for hair; white for shoe soles and socks; and pink flesh.

STEP 3 FITTING THE PANTS

Use a rounded, sturdy handle or dowel to bend pant legs at knee. Press with fingers to form knee shape.

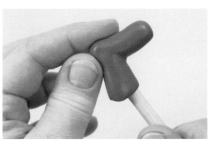

Use the dull edge of a knife or wooden blade to press in wrinkle marks.

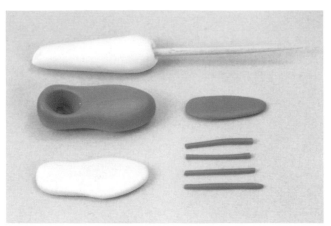

Repeat Step 4 for Studious Stan to fit Tess's pants, only position legs so that they bend back. Be sure to give some shape to Tess's backside.

STEP 4   SHOES AND SOCKS

For each of Tess's bright-pink tennis shoes (purchased for her sixth birthday by her Grandma Josie), roll a ½″-diameter ball. Use your fingers to press each ball into the shape of a shoe. For soles, roll a ⅜″ white ball. Flatten to ⅛″ thick, then press between fingers into a sole shape. For each sock, roll a 1¼″ × ⅜″ rope. Insert a toothpick into each sock—leave it long for now so that you have a handle to hold it.

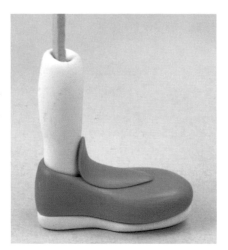

◄ Simulate shoestrings, lacing holes and tread the same as you did for Studious Stan, page 40. Be creative! You don't have to copy Tess's original shoes (though they *are* her favorites). Go into your closet, get a pair of your own sneakers and copy the stitch lines and tread.

Use a brush handle to hollow a space in the shoe for placing Tess's sock. Add sock. Place shoe on top of sole and press them together with your fingers. Add tongue, made from a ¼″ ball of pink that is shaped and flattened.

STEP 5   THE SECOND BAKE ►

Trim the toothpicks and sock ends so that her legs fit into her pant legs. Gently press pant legs against socks to bond. Place Tess's body on a baking pan. Prop her shoes against a ceramic coffee cup so that they won't droop in the oven, protecting her toes with a piece of kitchen parchment paper so that they don't get shiny from the cup surface. Bake for twenty minutes. Cool.

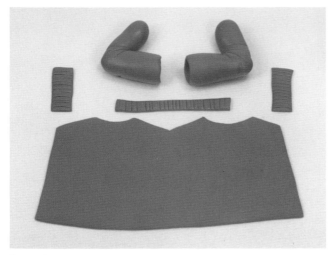

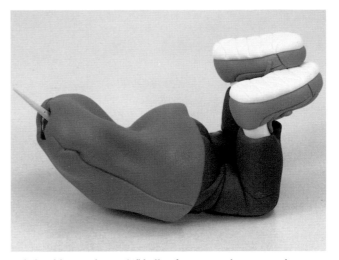

STEP 6 SHIRT AND ARMS

Cut the shirt and neck trim from a flattened magenta sheet, just as you did for Studious Stan. You will also need two smaller pieces for sleeve trim, since Tess is wearing a long-sleeve shirt. Press shirt with fabric for texture. Use a knife to cut ribbed lines into the trim. For each sleeve, roll a ⅜″ × 1¾″ rope. Hollow sleeve with a dowel or brush handle. Insert dowel into sleeve and bend sleeve at elbow.

Pad shoulders with two ⅜″ balls of magenta clay. Form shirt into a tube shape by overlapping short ends. Press overlapped ends with fabric to get a smooth seam. Slip shirt over body and overlap front shoulder piece over back shoulder piece. Position shirt sides, lifting with a brush to position folds, if necessary.

Make arms follow-
ing directions on
page 22. The arms,
including the
hands, begin with a
1½″ × ⅜″ rope.
Tess's hand is ½″
from fingertip to
wrist. Wrap cuff
trim around wrists
and position arms
in sleeves.

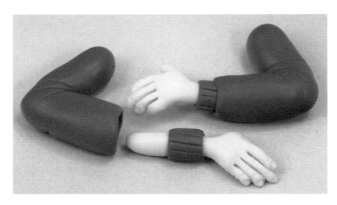

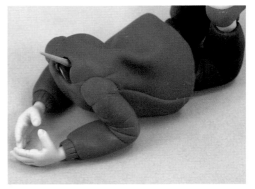

Press sleeves in place. Press with fabric to make shoulders smooth. Use a needle tool or dull edge to press in wrinkle lines.

◄ For Tess's neck, press a ½″ × ⅜″ rope in place. Position neck trim, overlapping in the back. Place an un-baked football into her hands.

STEP 7 FOOTBALL

To make the football, roll a 1″-diameter ball from caramel clay. Roll into an almond shape. Use a knife to cut in about six evenly spaced seam lines along the length of the ball. Press in four tiny Xs in a row for stitch marks.

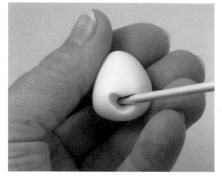

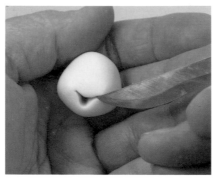

STEP 8   HEAD

Begin with a very smooth 1″-diameter ball. Roll into an egg shape. Use a blunt needle tool to press in a half-moon mouth—rolling the tool to keep the inside of the mouth very smooth. Notice that Tess's mouth is bigger than Suzette's.

Use your fingers to gently push up the corners and partially close the mouth. Press the corners in slightly with the tip of a knife. Soften the corners by stroking with the clay-brush tool.

Blend in a teardrop-shaped nose. Add eyes and eyelids.

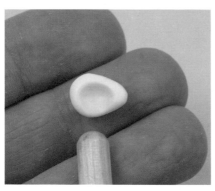

Shape ear from a ³⁄₁₆″ ball of clay. Hollow center with the round end of a dowel, and position onto head.

Press head onto toothpick neck and check its position and tilt. The "attitude" with which she carries her head determines much of her personality. Tess's hair is made like Stan's, using slightly longer pieces of black clay. Brush blush onto her cheeks and knuckles.

STEP 9   THE THIRD BAKE

Place Tess on a baking sheet with legs propped as they were before. Bake. Don't forget to play some loud and cheerful music to keep Tess's mind busy while she's in the oven. Let her cool before removing her from the oven.

Give Tess brown eyes, following directions for Sweet Suzette on page 36.

Playful Pete

Playful Pete loves to play games. His current favorite is marbles, but next week it might be soccer or jacks. He especially loves to play checkers in the park with Old Man Jones on those sunny afternoons when the weather seems perfect for lingering and visiting. Pete even beats him once in a while, which always makes Mr. Jones's eyes twinkle.

Pete's crossed legs are a little tricky. Be sure and do the first bake on this step to save yourself some frustration.

STEP 1   MIXING COLORS

To lighten Pete's shirt, mix seven parts light turquoise with one part white. His pants are seven parts turquoise green and one part white. His skin is equal parts flesh pink and caramel. For his gray shoes, mix three parts white with one part black. You will also need: a 1" ball of junk, or leftover clay for underwear; black for hair; white for socks; and transparent for marbles.

STEP 2   FROM UNDERWEAR TO THE FIRST BAKE

To make underwear, roll a 1" ball of junk clay into a cone shape. Stand the cone upright and insert a toothpick into the small end so that ½" remains exposed. Bake for twenty minutes. Cool.

From turquoise-green mix, roll a ¾"-diameter ball. Flatten it between your hands into a 2" diameter pancake shape. For legs, roll two ½"-diameter logs, each 2" long. Hollow legs to knees. Insert rounded dowel into leg and bend at knee. Use a blunt knife to press wrinkles around the knee area. Use your thumb to press the inside top thigh area of each pant leg flat.

STEP 3   FITTING THE PANTS

Press the pancake over the bottom of the cooled underwear. Blend the legs into the bottom of the underwear, using Step 4 for Studious Stan for guidance. Position legs so that they cross each other. Use the dowel tool to bend the legs into position.

STEP 4   SHOES AND SOCKS

Pete's shoes are just like Tess's, except his are gray. For each shoe, roll a ½"-diameter ball, then use your fingers to press each ball into the shape of a shoe. For soles, roll a ⅜" black ball. Flatten to ⅛" thick, then press into a sole shape.

For each sock, roll a 1¼" × ⅜" white rope. Insert a toothpick into each sock, leaving it long for now so that you have a handle for holding each sock.

Use a brush handle to hollow a space in the shoe for Pete's sock. Add sock. Place the shoe on top of the sole and press them together with your fingers. Add tongue, made from a ¼" gray ball that is shaped and flattened. Simulate shoestrings, lacing holes and tread the same as you did for Studious Stan. Once again, be creative! Add some stitch lines to Pete's shoes that make them different from Stan's or Tess's.

STEP 5   THE SECOND BAKE

Trim the toothpicks and sock ends so that Pete's legs will fit into his pant legs. Gently press pant legs against socks to bond. Place Pete's body on a baking pan. Bake for twenty minutes. Cool.

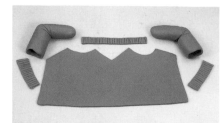

STEP 6   SHIRT

From a flattened light-turquoise sheet, cut shirt, neck trim and sleeve trim as you did for Tess. Press shirt with fabric for texture. Use a knife to cut ribbed lines into the trim. For each sleeve, roll a ⅜″ × 1¾″ rope. Hollow sleeves with a dowel or brush handle. Insert dowel into sleeve and bend sleeve at elbow.

Pad shoulders with two ⅜″ balls of light-turquoise clay. Form shirt into a tube shape by overlapping short ends. Press overlapped ends with fabric to get a smooth seam. Slip shirt over body, overlapping front shoulder piece over back shoulder piece. Use the claybrush tool to position the shirt.

STEP 7   ARMS AND NECK

Make arms following directions on page 22. The arms and hands begin with a 1½″ × ⅜″ rope. Pete's hand is ½″ from fingertip to wrist. Wrap cuff trim around wrists. Position arms in sleeves and press in place. Use a needle tool to press in wrinkles.

For his neck, press a ½″ × ⅜″ flesh rope over the toothpick. Overlap neck trim in back. Prop one hand over a piece of foil so that Pete is reaching out.

STEP 8   HEAD

Begin with a very smooth 1″-diameter ball. Roll into an egg shape. Use a blunt needle tool to press in a half-moon mouth—rolling the tool to keep the inside of the mouth smooth. Use your fingers to gently push up the corners and partially close the mouth. Press in the corners slightly with the tip of a blunt needle tool. Soften corners by stroking with the claybrush tool. Blend in a teardrop-shaped nose. Add eyes, eyelids and a ³⁄₁₆″ flattened ball for each ear.

STEP 9   THE THIRD BAKE

Press head onto toothpick neck. Pete is looking up and to his right. Experiment with the angle of his head and see what a difference it makes in his "mood." Brush some pink blush onto his cheeks. Place Pete on baking sheet and bake for twenty minutes. Cool.

STEP 10   HAIR

Now that Pete is hardened, you can easily pick him up as you style his hair. Make some very soft black clay by adding Mix Quick or another kneading medium to a ¾″ ball of black clay. My mix was three parts black to two parts Mix Quick. Flatten this ball and press it firmly over Pete's head, following his hairline. Use a needle tool to carve in tiny curls all over his head.

◄ STEP 11   MARBLES AND THE FOURTH BAKE

Pinch off three different colors from leftover, or junk, clay. Mix each color slightly with a ⅛″ ball of transparent clay, leaving the colors marbled. Place the marbles in Pete's outstretched hand.

Bake Pete, following manufacturer's directions. Let him cool in the oven.

◄ STEP 12 PAINTING THE EYES

Paint Pete's eyes brown. Brush a coat of FIMO lacquer on the marbles.

Mischievous Mike

Mischievous Mike never quite settles down. Even when he sleeps he dreams of the tricks he can play on the other neighborhood kids. He's never mean, though, which is why, even though he can be a real nuisance, the neighborhood ladies get a kick of looking out their windows to see what Mike is doing now. Mike has a jazzy white stripe added to his shirt, and his forward-leaning position requires more propping during baking than did the previous kids.

STEP 1   MIXING COLORS ►

To lighten Mike's clothing, mix one part white with seven parts of violet for his shirt, and with seven parts turquoise green for his pants. His bright red hair is four parts transparent mixed with one part magenta and one part golden yellow. You will also need a 1″ ball of junk, or leftover clay for underwear, black for shoes and white for socks.

STEP 2   FROM UNDERWEAR TO THE FIRST BAKE

To make underwear, roll a 1″ ball of junk clay into a cone shape. Stand the cone upright and insert a toothpick into the small end so that ½″ remains exposed. Lean the cone forward against a ceramic mug when you bake it so that it tilts. Prebake Mike's underwear for twenty minutes so that it is easier to form and position the pants. Cool.

From turquoise green clay, roll a ¾″-diameter ball. Flatten it between your hands into a 2″-diameter pancake shape. For legs, roll two ½″-diameter logs, each 1¾″ long. Hollow legs to knees. Insert a rounded dowel into each leg and bend at knee. Use a blunt knife to press wrinkles around knee area. Use your thumb to press the inside top thigh area of each pant leg flat.

STEP 3   FITTING THE PANTS

Press the pancake over the bottom of the cooled underwear. Blend the legs into the bottom of the underwear, using Step 4 for Studious Stan for guidance. Mike is leaning forward so as you position him onto some blocks of wood, bend him into that position.

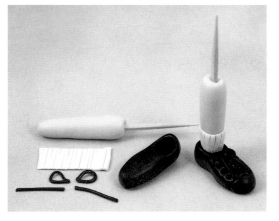

◄ STEP 4   SHOES AND SOCKS

Mike's shoes are just like Stan's, except they're black and he has worn off all of the tread with his racing around. The tongue is missing, too, so these are the easiest of the boys' shoes to make. For each shoe, roll a ½″-diameter ball, then use your fingers to press each ball into the shape of a shoe.

For each leg, roll a 1¼″ × ⅜″ rope. Insert a toothpick into each leg. For each sock, cut a ½″ × 1″ white strip. Cut in ribbing marks with a knife. Wrap sock loosely around the leg, trimming the back to fit. Use your finger to roll down one edge of each sock. Use the brush handle to hollow a space in the shoe for Mike's leg. Simulate shoestrings and lacing holes the same as you did for Studious Stan.

STEP 5 THE SECOND BAKE

Trim toothpick and top of leg so that the legs will fit into pant legs. Gently press pant legs against legs to bond. Place Mike and his blocks onto a baking sheet. Prop his body against a ceramic mug to keep him from tipping over as he gets hot and softens in the oven. Bake for twenty minutes. Cool.

Lay stripes over front of shirt. For texture, press shirt with a piece of fabric. (Laying the shirt on top of a piece of fabric while pressing will keep it from sticking to table.) Trim ends of stripes to fit.

STEP 6 SHIRT AND ARMS

From a flattened violet sheet, cut shirt and a ³⁄₁₆″ × 1¾″ strip for neck trim as you did for Pete. Use a knife to cut ribbed lines into trim. For each sleeve, roll a ⅜″ × 1¼″ violet rope. Hollow lower third of sleeve with dowel or brush handle. Bend sleeve over dowel to form elbow. For stripes, cut two 4″ × ⅛″ white strips.

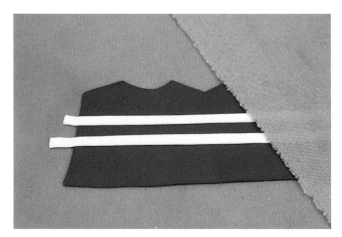

◄ Pad shoulders with two ⅜″ violet balls. Form shirt into a tube shape by overlapping short ends. Press overlapped ends with fabric to get a smooth seam. Slip shirt over body, overlapping front shoulder piece over back shoulder piece. Use the claybrush tool to position shirt.

► Press sleeves in place. Press shoulders with fabric to make them smooth. Use a needle tool or dull edge to press in wrinkle lines. Use a dowel to position sleeves in a reaching-up motion.

For Mike's neck, press a ½″ × ⅜″ flesh rope over the toothpick. Position neck trim, overlapping in the back.

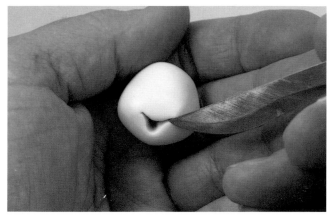

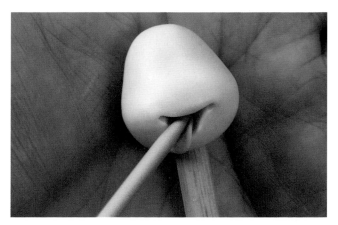

STEP 7   HEAD

Begin with a very smooth 1″-diameter ball. Roll into an egg shape. Use a blunt needle tool to press in a half-moon mouth—rolling the tool to keep the inside of the mouth smooth. Use your fingers to gently push up the corners and partially close mouth. Press in the corners slightly with the tip of a blunt needle tool or knife.

Blend in teardrop-shaped nose. Add eyes and eyelids, and a ³⁄₁₆″ flattened teardrop shape for each ear. Use the claybrush tool to soften and blend any harsh lines on the face.

For Mike's tongue, mix a ⅛″ flesh ball with a touch of magenta until evenly pink. Roll into a ball and then into a rounded teardrop. Flatten slightly. Pick up tongue with a blunt needle tool and position smaller end into mouth, rolling tool to loosen and position tongue.

STEP 8   HANDS AND HAIR

Press head onto the toothpick neck. Mike is looking up and slightly to his left. Make arms following directions on page 22. The arms, including the hands, begin with a 1½″ × ⅜″ rope. Mike's hand is ½″ from fingertip to wrist. Press arms into sleeves, trimming them to fit. Brush some pink blush on his cheeks and knuckles.

Flatten some of the orange-red mix into a 1″-wide strip. Cut this into a fringe, similar to that for Stan, and separate the strands by lightly rolling the end of each piece between your fingers. Style Mike's hair by adding a few pieces at a time.

STEP 9   THE THIRD BAKE

Prop Mike against two ceramic coffee mugs so that his arms remain upraised and he doesn't tip over. Keep the prop spots from getting shiny by placing a piece of kitchen parchment paper between the clay and the mug. Bake Mike, following the manufacturer's directions. Let him cool in the oven. (It's best to place him in the oven alone, as he's sure to tease other kids who are placed in there with him!)

STEP 10   PAINTING THE FACE

Paint Mike's eyes blue, following directions on page 36 for Sweet Suzette. Add freckles by lightly and quickly touching a liner brush, slightly damp with brown paint, to his cheeks. Too much paint on the brush will cause big blobs.

Gymnast Marissa

STEP 1   MIXING COLORS ▶

Marissa's hair is a mix of equal parts transparent, magenta and ochre. Her leotard is a blend of five parts white and one part magenta. You will also need pink flesh and white for her ruffle.

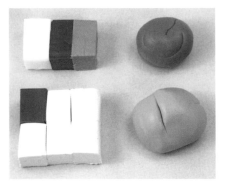

Gymnast Marissa, Mischievous Mike's little sister, is a natural-born performer. She loves anything that makes people clap, and currently she is getting the biggest applause for her tumbling tricks. Her ambition is to learn to tap like her Aunt Kathy, whom she adores.

Marissa's body is not baked until the legs, arms and ruffles are added. This means that you will need to "touch softly" so you don't leave fingerprints and misshapen bumps. You may find this the trickiest project in this chapter. So, every so often, make yourself a nice cup of tea and relax. You and Marissa will both perfect your skills with practice.

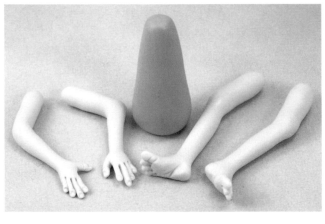

STEP 2 LEGS AND ARMS

Marissa's legs begin the same as Suzette's on page 32. If you need help, refer to those pictures. Roll two ¾″-diameter balls of flesh clay. Roll each into a smooth tube 2½″ long. Roll each leg between your fingers, at spots above and below the knee, to create a curved leg shape. Her feet are ¾″ long from heel to toe. (Bare feet instructions are on page 25.) Make arms and hands following directions on page 22. Marissa's arms are 2″ long (including her hands) and ⅜″ thick at the widest part. Her hand is ½″ from wrist to fingertip. For her leotard, roll a 1¼″ pink ball into a 2″-tall cone.

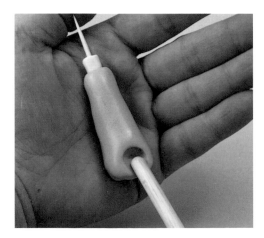

◀ STEP 3   POSITIONING NECK AND LEGS

Make a hole for her neck, using a round dowel tool or large paintbrush handle. Press a toothpick into the hole, leaving 1″ exposed. Press a ½″ × ⅜″ flesh-rope neck over the toothpick.

Press an indentation into the bottom sides of the cone at the spots where the legs will be attached. Try to hold lightly, like you would a hot potato, so that your fingerprints don't show. Holding with the curved palm of your hand instead of your fingers will also help.

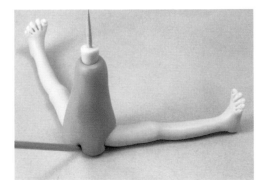

Press legs into a "splits" position. Hold the body by the toothpick as much as possible to eliminate fingerprints. If you do leave marks, *gently* smudge them away by rubbing with a lifting motion. Use a blunt needle tool to indent Marissa'a bottom. Soften the line with a claybrush tool.

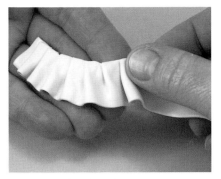

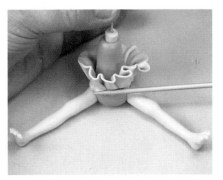

STEP 4 RUFFLES

To mix the pale-pink ruffle color, add a ⅝″ ball of leftover light pink to a ⅞″ ball of white clay. Flatten this into a long strip, 5″ × 1″. For the ruffle, use the pattern on page 37 to cut one piece 5″ × ¾″. For the bow, cut four pieces 1″ × ¼″.

To make ruffles, fold the long strip into numerous small pleats. These don't have to be perfectly even, as this is her practice uniform!

Place ruffle around her middle in an upside-down position, with pleats on the inside. Attach ruffle by pressing the bottom edge against her leotard with a blunt needle tool.

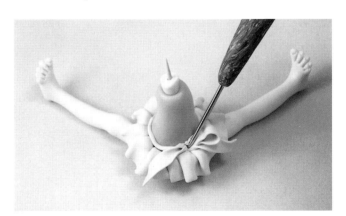

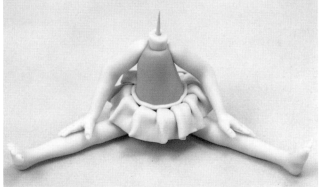

Flip ruffle down so that the pleats are now on the outside, covering the seam line. Use a soft brush to position pleats. To cover gaps around the waistline, roll a very thin pale-pink rope and lay it along the top of the ruffles. In the back, add the two tails and two loops for her bow, pressing them into place with a blunt needle tool.

STEP 5 ARMS AND THE FIRST BAKE

Position Marissa's arms, then press from opposite sides to bond both to her body. Rest her hands on her knees (bending them at the wrist at almost a right angle will make them look more relaxed). Set Marissa on the baking sheet, then make a final check of the position of her legs. If she feels at all unstable (don't we all!) prop her—front and back—with ceramic coffee mugs. Be sure to protect her from a shiny spot by positioning a piece of kitchen parchment paper between her and the mug. Bake for twenty minutes. Cool.

STEP 6 HEAD

Marissa's head is very similar to Suzette's, except her nose is slightly smaller and more upturned. Make her head—adding nose, eyes and eyelids—and place it on top of the toothpick. I positioned her looking almost straight ahead because she is trying not to lose her balance. Brush pink blush on her cheeks and knuckles.

STEP 7 HAIR

From a flattened sheet of the magenta and ochre mix, cut a strip 3″ × 1″. Cut this into as many ¹⁄₁₆″ × 1″ pieces as possible. Wrap one piece around the end of a needle tool in a spiral shape. Roll the needle tool against Marissa's head to loosen and position the curl. Continue placing curls until her head is covered.

STEP 8 THE FINAL BAKE AND PAINTING

Position Marissa on the baking pan, propping her once again, and bake according to the manufacturer's directions. Cool in oven. Paint her eyes and freckles as you did for her brother Mike.

Gentle Jess

Gentle Jess is kind. There is no other word that quite describes the way that she looks out for the other kids—and listens to their tales of woe and triumph. Even Mike, who is a great tease, is a little gentler when around Jess.

This chapter ends with Jess because her clothes are slightly more complicated than those of the other kids. This is especially for those of you who like intricate projects! But, if you have followed along one by one in making the other six, you will be familiar with each technique.

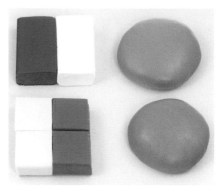

STEP 1   MIXING COLORS

Jess's skin is a mix of equal parts pink flesh and caramel. (For darker skin, use terra cotta clay instead of caramel, and cut the red tone by adding a pinch of navy blue.) Her dress is a mix of equal parts of white and blue. You will also need white for her underwear, blouse and socks, and black for her hair.

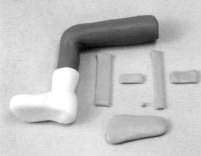

STEP 2   LEGS AND SOCKS

Jess's legs begin the same as Suzette's on page 32. If you need help, refer to those pictures. Roll two ¾″-diameter balls of caramel-flesh clay. Roll each into a smooth tube 2½″ long. Bend the tube softly in half, rolling above and below the knee to create a leg shape.

For sock cuff, cut two pieces approximately ½″ × ¾″ from flattened white clay. Wrap around ankle and trim back seam of sock so that the edges don't overlap. Roll ankle between fingers to smooth. For bottom part of sock, roll two ⅝″-diameter white balls. Shape with your fingers into a shoe shape. Use a brush handle to hollow out space for the ankle. Press ankle in place, then shape sock again.

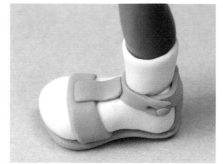

STEP 3   SANDALS

Mix the pale-blue sandal color by blending a ⅜″ ball of Jess's dress color with a ⅝″ ball of white clay. Each sole is a ⅜″ pale-blue ball flattened and shaped to match the bottom of her foot. Use the pattern on page 57 to cut the strap pieces from a flattened sheet of pale-blue clay.

Fit the sandal to the foot by laying the straps in place, beginning with the heel, then the top of the foot, the ankle strap and finally the short connector. Press Jess's foot onto the sole. To make the buttonhole, use the point of a knife to make a tiny slit in the end of the ankle strap. Press on a round blue-clay ball for a button.

STEP 4   UNDERWEAR AND THE FIRST BAKE

The pictures for making Suzette's underwear on page 32 will help you with the following steps. Roll a 1¼″-diameter ball of white clay into a 2½″-tall cone. Insert a dowel or sturdy brush handle halfway into the cone and hollow the cone until the opening is approximately 1¾″ wide. Place the cone over your thumb and bend at the halfway point. Jess is leaning back, so position the underwear leaning back onto the wooden bench, block of wood or other square ovenproof baking form. Insert legs into underwear, pressing underwear around legs to form a bond. Cross the legs at the ankle. If Jess's shoes need support, prop them on a crumpled foil ball. Bake for twenty minutes. Cool.

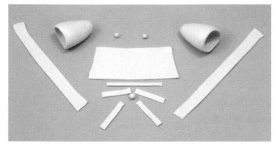

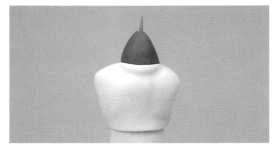

STEP 5   BLOUSE

From flattened white clay, cut blouse pieces using the pattern on page 57. For sleeves, roll two ⅝″ balls. Hollow each sleeve with a rounded dowel.

For neck, press a ½″ × ⅜″ flesh rope over the toothpick. Wrap the large blouse piece around Jess's chest, overlapping the ends in the back.

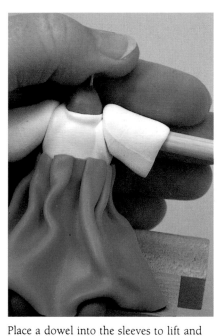

STEP 6   JUMPER

From flattened light-blue mix, cut the jumper pieces (pattern on page 57) and a 2″ × 6″ rectangle for the skirt. Press with fabric for texture.

Overlap the short ends of the skirt to create a tube. Slip over neck and position just above waist. Press soft gathers into the top of the skirt.

Place a dowel into the sleeves to lift and position them.

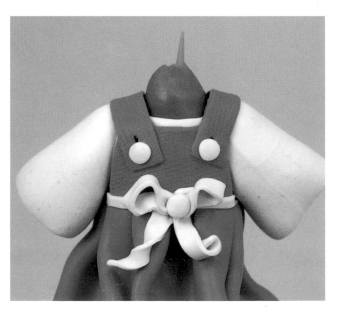

Add buttons and a white strip for front trim. Make the bow as you did for Marissa's ruffle, then twist tails slightly and curl under.

Now press the top of the jumper and the two blue straps in place. Make buttonholes with the tip of a knife.

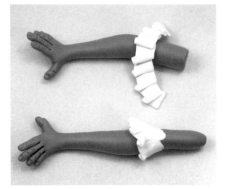

STEP 7 HANDS AND ARMS

Make arms and hands following directions in chapter three, page 22. Jess's arms are 1¾" long, including her hands, which are ½" from wrist to fingertip. Her hands are bent at almost right angles to her wrists so that she can lean backward on them.

To make sleeve ruffles, fold soft pleats into the two remaining long white strips. Wrap ruffles around arms. Roll the top of the arm between your fingers to compress the ruffles.

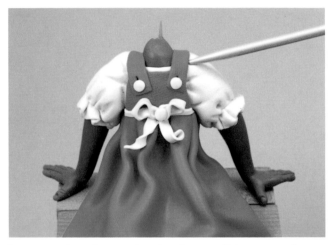

Insert arms into sleeves, trimming the arms if they are too long. Use a blunt needle tool to press wrinkle marks into the sleeves. This also helps to firmly attach the arms. Use a soft brush to lift and position the ruffles.

STEP 8 HEAD

Roll a 1"-diameter caramel-flesh ball for Jess's head. Make her mouth as you did Tess's, then close to a smile. Add her nose, eyes and eyelids. Brush pink blush on cheeks and knuckles.

STEP 9 THE SECOND BAKE

Prop Jess against a ceramic coffee cup to keep her from tipping over. Bake for twenty minutes. Cool.

STEP 10 HAIR

Because Jess is baked, you can now pick her up as you style her hair. From black clay, roll a 1" ball. Flatten this ball and press it over Jess's head, molding it into the shape of her haircut. Use a knife to cut in marks to simulate hair strands, as shown. Be orderly about it so that her part is straight! Bake, once again propping her against the ceramic mug. Let her cool in the oven.

STEP 11 PAINTING THE EYES

Paint eyes following directions for Suzette on page 36, except make Jess's brown.

Patterns

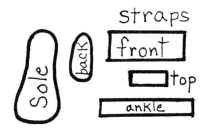

straps

front

top

ankle

back

Sole

Pattern for Jess's sandal.

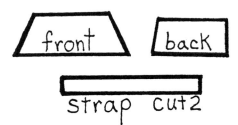

front

back

strap cut2

Pattern for Jess's jumper.

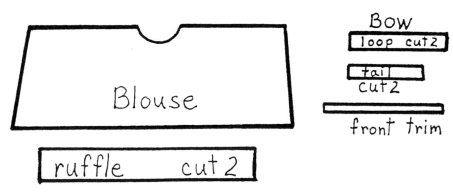

Blouse

ruffle cut 2

BOW

loop cut2

tail
cut2

front trim

Pattern for Jess's blouse.

CHAPTER SIX

The People Next Door: Creating Lifelike Faces

Characters, real characters at least, have lots of lines in their faces—and unusual noses and interesting mouths. It's hard to get those kinds of features with the simple techniques learned in the previous chapter. So in this chapter you'll learn how to add those extra lines and wrinkles that make someone a *real* personality.

The hardest character faces for me to make are breathtaking beauties, so we're going to leave breathtaking out of this chapter and concentrate on whimsical instead. Humor is very forgiving! And there is never an absolute right or wrong. I like those odds when I'm learning something new.

My principal goal in this chapter is to teach you specific face-sculpting techniques. I am not trying to teach you to make exact clones of my people, so don't get all hung up with tedious measuring for each facial feature. If the size of a certain nose looks good to you, then it is perfect for that particular character.

I will be showing you each step in detail for William Gregory, then fewer steps for Margaret Joyce and Randy John. You'll have lots of opportunities to practice the basic steps as you follow along with me. And remember, if a character doesn't turn out the way you planned, just change his name and give him a different story. I believe that's an acceptable path to success. Relieved? Let's begin. . . .

READYING THE CLAY

I chose clay colors for The People Next Door that I enjoy working, and living, with. I found this color scheme in a favorite children's book and copied the colors. This meant that I did a lot of mixing to get the custom tones, but, since color is a major part of each character's statement, I felt that the time spent was worth it. A piece of patterned fabric, a hotel carpet, flowers in the garden and greeting cards are other sources of inspiration.

I usually mix up just a small ball of each blend as a color check before committing myself to a whole batch. Too often I've done a whole character and then hated the colors. To mix colors, chop each color mix together in a food processor, as explained in chapter three. Then knead and twist until the clay is a uniform color. You can, of course, mix totally by hand, though it will take much longer. Either way, give yourself a whole evening to mix the colors.

To make the clay very elastic and moldable for models pictured, I added approximately one part (20 percent) Mix Quick kneading medium to every four parts (80 percent) FIMO. If the clay is too soft, it will fingerprint very easily and will droop and stretch, thus creating thin, weak spots. If it is too stiff, it will crack along the edge of the folds. Like Goldilocks, I want it "just right!"

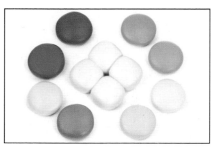

To lessen the intensity of the clay colors, I mixed each of the pictured base colors with four parts champagne FIMO.

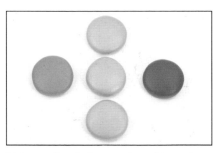

Lighter-colored clays, such as this apricot FIMO, can also be used to lessen the intensity of a given color. I mixed one part deep-magenta clay to three parts apricot to achieve this delightful salmon color.

The flesh mix for The People Next Door is four parts FIMO flesh mixed with one part FIMO caramel. It will darken somewhat as it bakes.

ROLLING SHEETS OF CLAY

To make the shirts, sweater and dress you will need thin (1/16″–1/8″ thick) sheets of well-conditioned clay from which to cut the patterns. Use either a rolling pin or a pasta machine to get a uniform thickness (see chapter three).

BAKING

All characters in this chapter are baked in stages to make them easier to handle. Read the clay package for the manufacturer's baking recommendations for the specific clay you are using. For strength, bake at the highest and longest recommended temperature and time.

During the final bake, I will sometimes leave the character in the oven longer than recommended (but never at a higher temperature) to make sure that all parts of it are equally cured. Then I let it cool in the oven after turning off the heat, to allow for a little extra bake time. I try not to skimp on the bake time—especially with these larger, more time-intensive characters. They are too much fun—and too much work—to have my efforts be destroyed due to a weak, underbaked product. The characters are very fragile while hot, so any shifting of position once they are in the oven is asking for trouble.

Note that most accessories need to be prebaked before adding them to the figures. Decide which accessories you'll give each figure before you begin the project, then check to see if they need to be prebaked—if so, you may want to make these first.

PLANNING THE PROJECT

Because the characters in this chapter are a family, you need to be sure that they will look like a family once they are done. This requires continual measuring and comparing, as it is very easy for them to grow and change as you are working. (I've had some students whose work would no longer fit in the oven!)

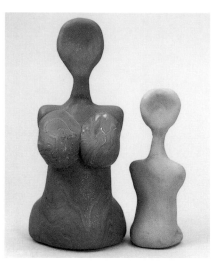

When working on a grouping, check frequently to see that the sizes and body shapes are correct for the pieces you have in mind.

Even at this stage, the pieces look like father, mother and child.

Remember, though, that the people in this chapter are caricatures; thus, we are not bound by set body proportions. Body proportions are often measured in comparison with the height of one's head; since William's head is 2″ tall and he would stand about 10″ tall, we can figure that it would take about five of his heads stacked on top of each other to equal his height. Compare this with the average male, who is 7½ to 8 heads tall. It's this shorter body and larger head that gives our clay characters their whimsical and cartoonish appeal.

All three characters in this chapter start with a foil armature, which will give some support and fill up bulky center spaces. This reduces the amount of clay you will have to buy, plus decreases the likelihood of surface cracks caused by uneven heating of thick pieces.

William Gregory

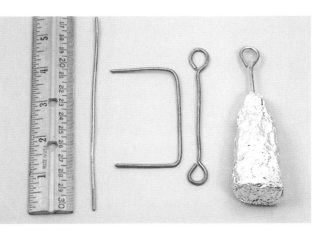

William Gregory is fun to be around because he has never really grown up. That fits well for his occupation as a writer of children's books. It doesn't sit quite so well with his wife Margaret Joyce, who has been trying to get him to build bookshelves for her growing library. But, what can we expect of a man with so many interests? We all know that a bowling ball pulls more weight than a hammer, right? Will has been trying to find some time to take his son Randy fishing, but on a nice day the tennis courts sure look inviting. . . .

STEP 1   MAKING AN ARMATURE FOR SITTING CHARACTERS

For William's spine, cut a piece of wire 5½″ long. Bend 1½″ at each end into a right angle. Use round-nose pliers to turn each end into a circle. These circles will serve to hold the wire steady inside the body. Crumple a sheet of foil into a cone shape, embedding the wire in the center with 1″ protruding for the neck and head. Roll the cone on the table until the outside is smooth, making it easier to cover it with clay.

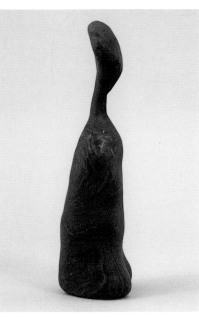

Flatten a sheet of junk clay to ⅛″ thick. Cover the armature with this sheet, smudging seams to blend edges. Press between your palms to smooth and shape surfaces. Form clay over head armature into a thick spoon shape, keeping neck thin. Shape body with hips, shoulders and waist.

STEP 2   THE FIRST BAKE

If he is lumpy now, the lumps may show through his clay clothes later on—just like with real people! Do you want him to have a potbelly or a tilted head? If so, shape the armature that way. Bake the armature for thirty minutes. Cool.

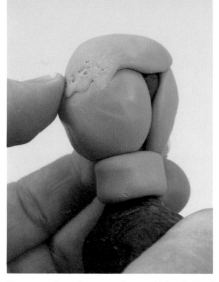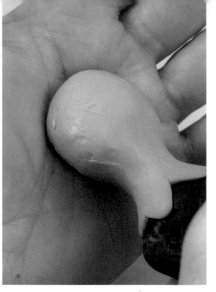

STEP 3   SCULPTING A HEAD
Press a 1" ball of flesh clay onto the face of the armature. Flatten three 1" balls. Press one onto top of head, one over the back of head and one around the neck.

Use your thumb to smudge and blend all of the seams.

Press and roll the head between your palms to even and smooth the surface.

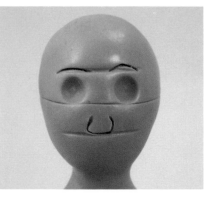

Now mark the face into thirds; your halfway mark should be at the center of your middle third. Draw in the eyebrows on the top line. Draw the bottom of the nose on the bottom line.

Check the profile of the head. From the side you should be able to see that the back of the head bulges out slightly just above the neck. The front of the face is fairly straight. No part of the head is flat; rather, it is rounded like an egg. (Though he may act like it sometimes, Will is *not* a blockhead.)

Use a needle tool to mark a line halfway down on the front of the face. Roll a round tool, such as the clay handle on your needle tool, into each eye socket. For an adult like William, this is just above the halfway line. There should be room between the eyes for another eye.

Make two lines that divide the bottom third of the face into thirds. Draw the top of the mouth on the first of the two lines you just made. Use a large needle tool, such as a no. 2 knitting needle, to begin a large mouth hole. Roll the tool to smooth the interior edges.

STEP 4 LIPS

Each lip is made from a ⅜″ ball that is rolled into a teardrop shape, then pressed between your fingers into a flat triangular shape. Now flatten the top five-sixths of the triangle, leaving the bottom edge thicker. This slightly thick ridge will become Will's upper lip. Repeat this shape for the lower lip.

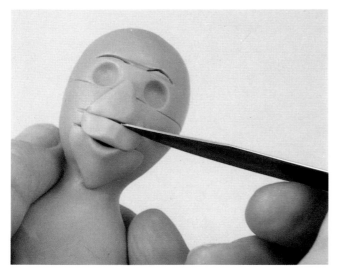

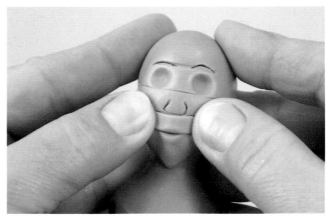

Use your thumbs to blend the edges of the triangles into the face. Draw the corners back so that the mouth begins to curve around the egg shape.

Position the lower lip so that it completely covers the bottom edge of the mouth hole. Stretch the corners of the lip slightly upward. Now position the upper lip so that it covers the upper edge of the hole. Pull the corners down slightly so that they overlap the corners of the bottom lip. Trim the top of the triangle at the nose line.

STEP 5 NOSE

The nose begins with a ⅜″ ball, which is rolled into a teardrop shape and then pressed between your fingers into a pyramid. Continue to pat this pyramid into a tiny nose shape. The nose is tilted to the left in the picture so that you can see that the tip is rounded.

Try Will's nose on for size. (On him, not you!) Set it on the nose line and stand back and look at it. Is it too big? Too small? If so, make it over. Use the needle tool to indent a groove just above the lip.

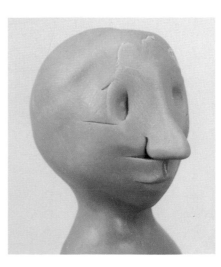

Use your thumbs to blend the nose into the cheek, forehead and eye area.

STEP 6   CHEEKS ▶

Each cheek is formed from a ½″-diameter ball, which is rolled into a long teardrop, turned into a comma shape and flattened. The thickness of this cheek piece greatly affects the look of the face. Experiment with different thicknesses to see what looks best to you.

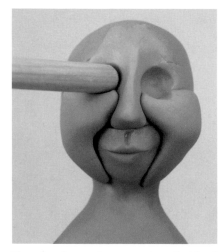

Place one flattened comma on each side of the nose. The point where the comma touches the nose—just above the flare of the nostrils—should be quite flat. Roll a round tool into the eye socket to shape the bridge of the nose and to indent the cheek just below the eyes.

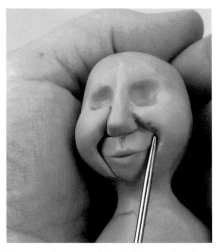

Use your fingers to blend the outside edges of the cheeks into the sides of the head. Press a blunt needle tool gently along the inside edge of the cheek to begin to blend it into the face. It's OK on caricatures to leave this line rather exaggerated.

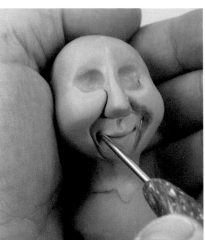

Use the blunt needle tool to deepen the corners of the mouth. Get a hand mirror and set it beside you while you work. (Come on, do it. This really does help.) Smile at yourself in the mirror. Notice how your lips meet the curves of your cheeks. The bigger your smile is, the more recessed the corners become, because they are drawn around the curve of your teeth.

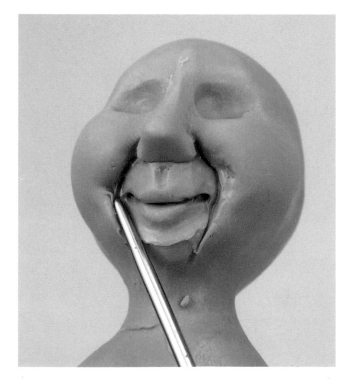

◀ You may now be left with an indentation that looks gouged. Gently smooth this by pulling the extra clay into the chin area. Work to keep it smooth. The action feels a bit like smoothing putty with a trowel.

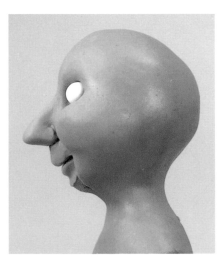

Indent the nose at the eye line. Press two prebaked eyes in place. These should be deeper than the bridge of the nose. Check Will's profile. What's missing? I think he needs a chin and forehead. He's cute, but weaker in character than I imagine my neighbor Will to be.

To make his forehead protrude more, add a forehead piece. Roll a ⅝″ ball into a flattened oblong. Roll your dowel or brush handle against one long side to create indentations for the eyes.

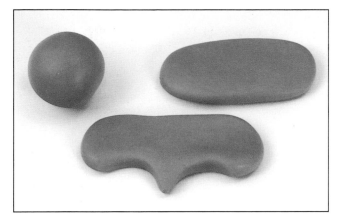

Position this piece above the eyes. Does it stick out too far? If so, remove and flatten it. Too small? Remove it and make a bigger one. For the chin, make a piece that looks like a sports chinstrap that is thick in the middle. Place this over Will's chin, stretching the ends along the jaw line.

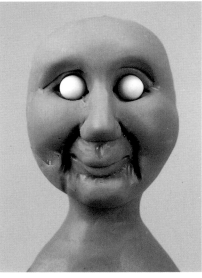

Use your fingers and the blunt needle tool to blend the seams into the face. Don't push too hard or you'll flatten out what you just added!

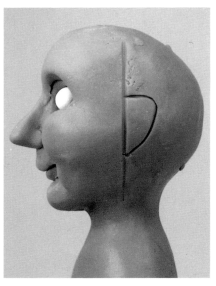

Check his profile again. He has a really receding lower lip; shall we leave it that way? Perfect regularity can be boring, so let's just proceed. Mark the side of the head along the center line. Draw in the ear to correspond with lines from the upper eyelid and upper lip.

STEP 7   EARS

Form the ears from ⅜″ balls of clay that become teardrops, then flattened kidney shapes. Roll the rounded dowel end into the center of each, leaving a ridge along three sides.

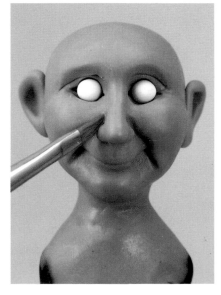

Position the ears by using a rounded tool to press the center of each into the head. Return to any rough spots and pat and smudge to smooth them. Use the claybrush tool to smooth along seam lines where your fingers cannot reach. Press brush along sides of nose to accentuate nostrils.

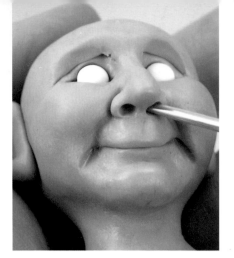

Use a blunt needle tool to press holes for nostrils. Lift the tool to the side to flare out the nostrils.

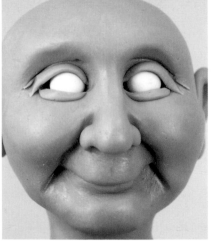

STEP 8   EYELIDS

Add flat comma shapes for eyelids. Try them on before blending. Too big? Too small? Fat lids will make him look like he cried all night. The upper lid usually overlaps the bottom one slightly. Be sure to leave a space at the corners of the eyes for tears to flow. Check the side profile. The outside corner of the eye shows in the side view.

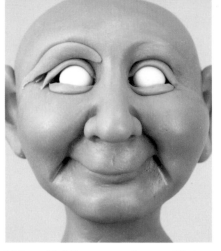

Make a third flat comma shape to fill the gap between the upper eyelid and the eyebrow. Check out the real people around you. (Not too obviously, please! Some of my students have been accused of staring in restaurants after being at one of my classes.) I'm continually intrigued by the different shapes of lids, wrinkles, brow bones and under-eye bags.

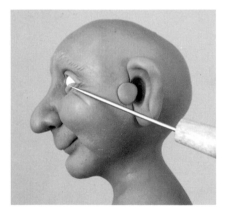

Place a small ball of clay just in front of the ear. If the face is the way you want it now, press wrinkles around the eyes with a thin needle tool. I press and lift the tool so that the wrinkle lines curve over the cheeks. Draw in eyebrows with a thin needle tool.

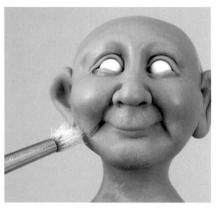

Use the needle tool and brush to blend the ear area. A little waterless hand cleaner on the brush will smooth rough areas. But don't do this until the last step, as it will make the surface sticky. Use a stiff stencil brush to push in whisker marks.

STEP 9   THE SECOND BAKE

Give him a last-minute checkover, then brush on blush for cheek coloring. If the surface is sticky from the waterless hand cleaner, let surface dry before applying blush. Bake for thirty minutes. Cool.

STEP 10   PAINTING THE EYES

Paint the eyes with acrylic paint, following general directions for Sweet Suzette on page 36. I painted Will's eyes brown, but you can do whatever you like.

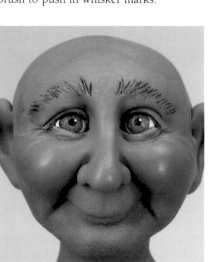

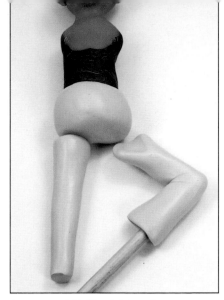

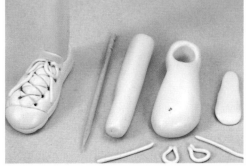

STEP 12   SHOES AND SOCKS

His shoes begin with a ⅞"-white ball that is then formed into a shoe shape. Use the dowel to hollow a space for the ankle. For the sock, roll a 2" × ⅜" rope. Press a toothpick through the center of the sock to give stability to his ankle. Fit sock into shoe. Press tongue in place. Follow directions for Studious Stan (page 40) to make stitch marks and shoelaces. Clip off excess toothpick and press sock firmly into pant legs.

STEP 11   MAKING PANTS

Will's clothes are made like those in chapter five, except bigger. First, a pancake is pressed over the bottom of the armature. To determine the length of the legs, roll clay ropes and lay in place as if he were standing. Hollow legs to knees, bending at that point. Press in a flat spot on the inside thigh.

Blend legs into pants bottom, making sure they are firmly attached. Place Will on a foil-covered, square-edged baking pan set on a baking sheet. If his feet don't rest on the bottom, support them with a foil pillow.

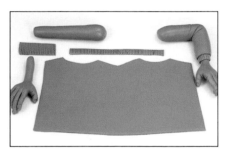

STEP 13   SHIRT AND HANDS

From a sheet of flattened blue clay, cut shirt pattern. Cut narrow strips for neck and sleeve trim. Each arm is a 2¼" rope, hollowed to the elbow. To add texture to all pieces, press with fabric. His hands, made following directions in chapter four, are 1⅓" from fingertip to wrist. Wrap sleeve cuff around wrist before adding hand to sleeve.

Pattern for William's shirt.

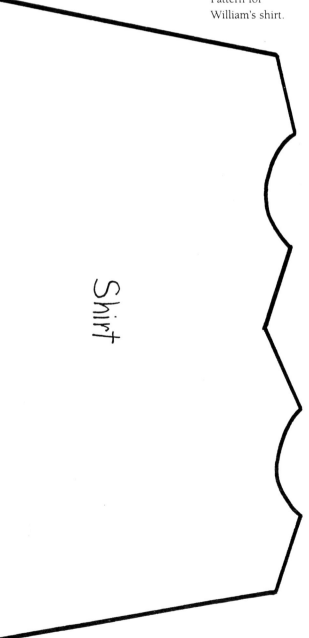

Shirt

To pad shoulders, blend a ½" ball of clay into each shoulder. Form shirt into a tube and slip over head. Adjust wrinkles with a soft brush.

Add sleeves simultaneously by pressing them against the body from opposite sides. Lay neck trim in place. Press shoulders and elbows with fabric. Position hands to hold accessories.

STEP 14   ACCESSORIES

Add customized accessories to his hands. To protect their shapes, all of the pictured accessories were baked before adding them to the figure. By changing the accessories, you can personalize a character—a great idea for gifts.

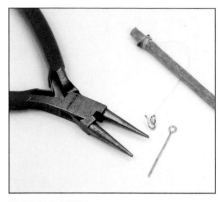

FISHING POLE

Cut a smooth stick that resembles a bamboo rod. Cut a jewelry-supply eye pin to ½″ in length. Use round-nose pliers to curve the end up like a hook. Tie the hook onto the pole with thread. Secure thread ends by dabbing with white glue. (It isn't necessary to bake the fishing pole as long as it can be slipped back in later.)

STEP 15   HAIR AND THE THIRD BAKE ▸

To make a base for Will's hair, press a 1½″-wide black clay pancake firmly onto head. From flattened 1″-wide strips of black clay, cut pieces resembling fringe. Add a few pieces at a time to style hair. Bake. Let cool in oven.

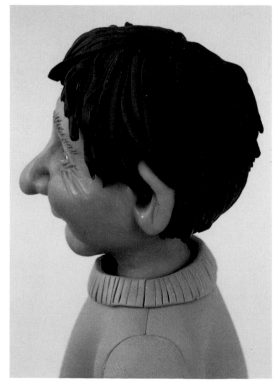

BOWLING BALL

Form a ¾″ foil ball and cover with a black clay pancake. Roll firmly to smooth. Use a sharp needle tool to press in three holes. Enlarge holes with larger tool. Bake. Cool. Brush on a coat of FIMO gloss lacquer. The half-lacquered ball at left shows what a difference the lacquer makes.

HAMMER

Press a 1″ brown rope into the shape of the handle. Bake. Cool. Press a gray clay ball firmly onto the small end of the handle. Form the hammer head from a ball of gray clay. Use a knife to cut in the nail-pulling prongs. Press head onto handle. Bake a second time.

TENNIS RACQUET

Cut an oval piece of window screen. Roll a 2¼″ × 3/16″ rope. Insert a toothpick through center of rope. Press a second piece of rope around the oval screen. Press screen securely to the small end of the handle. Bake. Cool. To simulate tape around the handle, roll a ⅛″ wide rope. Flatten. Wrap around bottom of handle. Press gold trim firmly over the edge of the screen and around the handle. Bake a second time.

Margaret Joyce

Margaret Joyce is currently on a health kick. It's salads every night for supper, and herbal tea instead of coffee. She has been doing research at the library on medicinal plants that are easy to grow indoors and on nutritious foods to lower cholesterol and hypertension. But, lest you think her reading is all serious, note that there are some romance novels tucked in there under those heavy medical volumes.

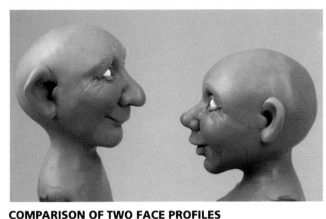

COMPARISON OF TWO FACE PROFILES

Margaret Joyce is sculpted with the same basic pieces as her husband, Will. But if you look carefully, you will see that slight variations in size and placement of the pieces make each character unique.

STEP 1   ARMATURE AND THE FIRST BAKE

Margaret's spine starts with a 5″ wire, bent at each end into small circles and then embedded into a crumpled foil cone.

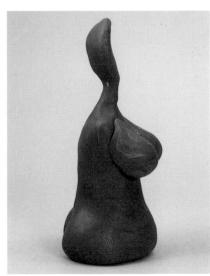

Flatten a sheet of junk clay to ⅛″ thick. Cover the armature with this sheet, smudging seams to blend edges. Form head into a thick spoon shape, leaving neck very thin. Add extra clay to those spots where Margaret is well padded.

If Margaret is uneven now, she will be uneven with her clothes on—so check body from all angles to be sure that it will fit your image of Margaret. Bake the armature for thirty minutes. Cool.

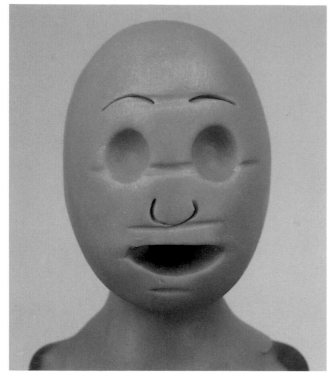

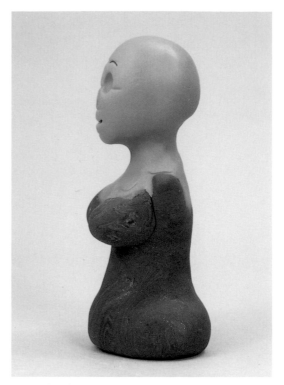

STEP 2   SCULPTING A HEAD

Form head shape the same as you did for William (page 62). Use a needle tool to mark the halfway line on the front of the face. Use a round tool to mark each eye socket. Now mark the face into thirds. Draw in the eyebrows on the top line. Draw the nose on the bottom line. Mark the bottom third of the face into thirds. Draw in the mouth on the top of those two lines. Use a large needle tool, such as a no. 2 knitting needle, to press in a large mouth. Roll the tool to smooth the interior edges.

Notice that, because Margaret's head is rounded like an egg and not flat like a square, some of the front facial lines still show in the profile view. See also how the back of her neck slopes up to the bulge of her head.

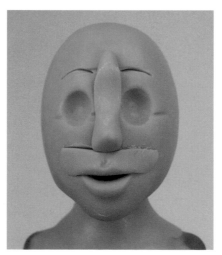

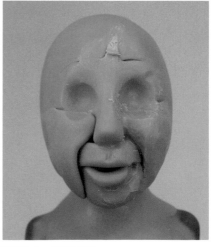

Make all of the add-on facial features in the same way you did for William. How big should each be? Try them on Margaret just as you would try on clothing in a store. Too big? Try another. Too small? Put it back. Remember that you can alter the shapes once you begin to blend and sculpt.

STEP 3   LIPS AND NOSE

Position the lower lip so it covers the bottom edge of the mouth hole. Stretch the corners slightly upward. Now position the upper lip. Pull the corners down to overlap the corners of the bottom lip. Trim the top of the triangle at the nose line. Position the nose, indenting it even with the eyes.

STEP 4   CHEEKS

Use your thumbs to blend the nose into the face. Add the cheek pieces. Roll a rounded tool into the eye sockets to indent the tops of the cheeks.

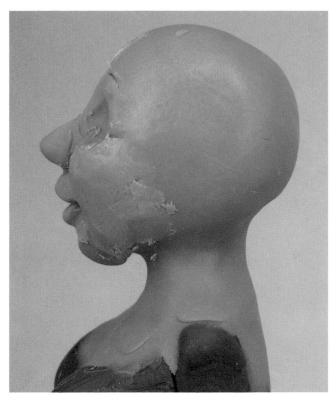

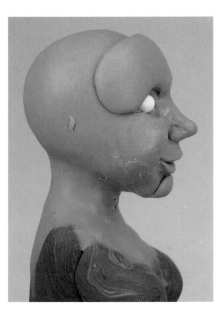

Add the extra pieces, checking them for size. Push the eyes into place. Notice that the individual steps don't need to be completely smoothed and finished before going on to the next step. I move continually over the face, adjusting here and there. No one feature is just right until it is *all* just right, as each feature is a part of the whole. Continue to blend and adjust. Take some away here; add some there. Deepen the corners of her mouth. Be sure to blend the chin so that the fullness of her bottom lip is retained.

Check Margaret's profile. What's missing? Margaret has more determination than Will, so let's give her a stronger chin. She also needs more brow bone, so we'll add a forehead piece. Notice that her lips are fuller and more evenly matched than Will's are.

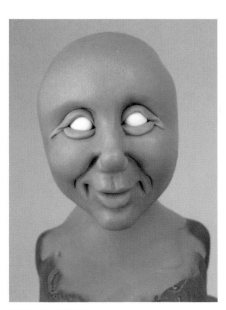

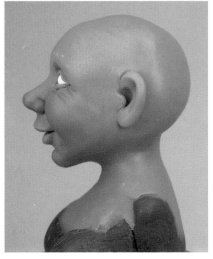

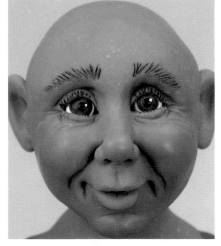

STEP 5   EYES

Use the claybrush tool to smooth the crease lines. Add flattened commas for eyelids. Mark corners of eyes. Deepen grin creases at corner of mouth, pushing with the claybrush to leave soft, not sharp, marks.

STEP 6   FINISHING THE HEAD

Check her profile again. Trim away excess eyelid. Smooth jawline. Check curve of nose and lips and bridge of nose—all areas where women tend to be curvier than men. Form the ears and position them just behind the halfway line of the side of the head. Check placement from the side and the front. Do final smoothing. Draw in eyebrows with a thin needle tool. If all is to your liking, add blush.

STEP 7   THE SECOND BAKE

Do a final check, then place Margaret in the oven and bake for thirty minutes. Cool.

STEP 8   PAINTING THE EYES

Paint the eyes the same as you did for Sweet Suzette (page 36). You can be creative with the color—try using a darker shade around the outside edge of the iris.

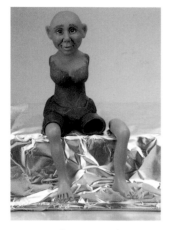

STEP 9 MAKING BLOOMERS AND LEGS

Yes, old-fashioned bloomers for Margaret. Actually, the practical reason is that this will give more stability to Margaret's legs. There isn't always a tight bond when unbaked clay is pressed against baked clay, so I feel safer knowing that Margaret's legs are locked into bloomers. I have lost legs, after baking, because I didn't attach them securely.

Margaret's legs, made following directions in chapter four, are 4″ long. Her feet are 1⅜″ from toe to heel. Bend her leg at the knee, smoothing and rolling at the knee to make a graceful leg. Add bloomers and legs following techniques for Randy's shorts (page 77).

STEP 10 DRESS

For Margaret's skirt, from a flattened clay sheet cut a 4″ × 8″ rectangle. Press with fabric for texture. Form into a tube by overlapping short ends. Slip over Margaret's head and press into gathers at her waist. Position folds with a soft brush. Firmly press ½″ balls of clay onto her shoulders to give added stability to sleeves.

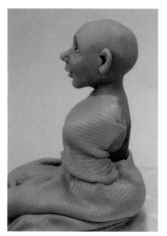

For Margaret's shirt, use the pattern for the sweater back and cut just one piece. Press with fabric for texture. Softly fold under the bottom edge and place over Margaret's chest. Press the shirt firmly to Margaret's shoulders.

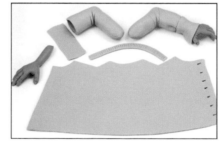

STEP 11 SWEATER AND HANDS

Cut pattern from a sheet of clay. Press in buttonholes. Each sleeve begins with a 2¼″ × ⅝″ rope. Hollow rope to elbow. Bend elbows. The hands, made following directions in chapter four, are 1¼″ long from fingertip to wrist. Insert hand into sleeve. Press cuff over bottom of sleeve.

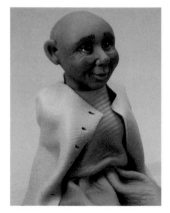

Position sweater over Margaret's shoulders, overlapping front shoulder over back.

Sweater

Pattern for Margaret's sweater.

STEP 13   SANDALS

Make sole pieces that will fit Margaret's feet. Try them on to be sure the size is right. Cut narrow strips for straps. (Boy, that's sure a tongue twister!)

Add sleeves simultaneously by pressing them against the body from opposite sides. Turn back cuffs. Place prebaked accessories (such as the bowl and spoon shown here) into her hands. Do this as soon as possible after making hands, as they should still be warm and pliable enough to position. Sometimes, if the clay is stiff and cold, the fingers will break if you try to reposition them. Press shoulders into a natural rounded shape. Be sure that the arms look as if there are actually straight arm bones inside those sleeves. Pat with fabric to re-move fingerprints.

STEP 12   THE THIRD BAKE

Lay neck trim in place, pressing gently. Press on tiny clay buttons. Bake for thirty minutes. Cool.

Lay straps firmly over feet. Now you will see why we baked the feet before adding sandals! Press the "cork" cushions in place, and then the soles. Smooth edges.

◄ STEP 14   THE HAIR

Flatten a ¾″ ball of black clay. Press firmly onto Margaret's head, keeping it slightly smaller than Margaret's hairline. Roll a long, flat black strip approximately 1½″ wide. Cut fringe into one long side of strip. Twist the pieces of fringe, then press into the base layer to style her hair.

STEP 15   THE SALAD ►

To make lettuce, roll small green clay balls. (The color will be even more realistic if you partially mix together transparent and leaf-green clays.) Press balls extremely flat. Rip into halves or thirds and drop into bowl. For white chunks, roll a ¼″ transparent clay rope. Cut into slices and chunks. For mush-room pieces, mix together white and cham-pagne for an off-white color. Roll a rope and cut slices. Last, add the cheese, which is yel-low clay grated through a piece of window screen.

STEP 16   THE FINAL BAKE

Bake for thirty minutes. Cool in oven. Set Margaret Joyce on a shelf, with her books and a favorite plant arranged beside her.

▶ **The Bowl.** Roll a ¾″-diameter gray clay ball. Hollow out the bowl center. An easy way to evenly hollow out the bowl is to roll a smooth, round shape against it. I searched my craft supply box for just the right tool, and used the head from a wooden people peg. Bake, then paint with FIMO gloss lacquer.

◀ **STEP 17   OTHER ACCESSORIES**

The Spoon. Roll a 2″ × ³⁄₁₆″ rope. Flatten one end slightly, then taper to a ball shape at the smaller end. Indent bowl of spoon. An easy way to get the right shape is to roll the rounded end of a dowel against the spoon tip. Bake. To keep the curve of the spoon handle from flattening out as it bakes, lay it across a fluff of flame-retardant polyester fiberfill (used for stuffing soft toys and pillows). Brush with FIMO matte lacquer when cool.

The Plant. The pot begins as a ¾″ rust clay ball made by mixing equal parts of magenta and caramel FIMO. Roll this into the shape of a tapered pot. For the dirt, flatten a ³⁄₈″ caramel clay ball to fit the top of the pot. Roughen the surface of the dirt. Press a hole into its center. Lay the dirt on top of the pot. Use a needle tool to press a hole to the bottom of the pot. Wrap a ¼″-wide rust strip around the top of the pot.

To make leaves, flatten ¼″ green clay balls between your fingers into a leaf shape. Press leaves between two real leaves to imprint texture and lines. Wrap bottom of leaf around a 2″ piece of green cloth-covered florist wire. Repeat for as many leaves as desired. Bake leaves and pot. Make tendrils by wrapping the florist wire around a needle tool.

After the leaves and pot are cooled, gather all of the wires together and arrange in the hole in the pot.

The Books. For the covers, cut a variety of colors of flat clay rectangles, ranging from 1″ × 2″ to 1½″ × 3″. For the pages, flatten several chunks of white clay in thicknesses ranging from ⅛″ to ⁵⁄₁₆″. Cut pages slightly smaller than one-half the length of the covers. Imprint page lines with your knife. Put pages inside covers. Press along the back edge of the book to create a binding line. Bake.

Randy John

Randy John is particularly fond of my peanut butter cookies, so of course I keep the cookie jar full—and I see him often. He's a cheerful, friendly sort of kid who always leaves me with a smile on my face. Just yesterday he was sharing with me his delight at getting ready to go on a camping vacation with his folks. I'll miss him while he's gone; I'll even miss his big slobbery dog, Mutt Lee.

Look carefully at the pictures of Randy John to see what it is that makes him look like a child instead of an adult. *Hint:* Notice the position of the eyes.

STEP 1 ARMATURE ▶

Randy's spine starts with a 4″ wire, bent at each end into small circles and then embedded into a crumpled foil cone. Keep foil very small. Keep measuring his body against the other characters so you don't end up with three adult figures.

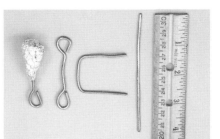

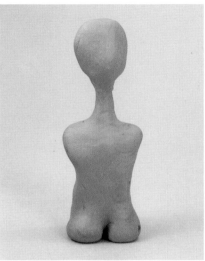

STEP 2 THE FIRST BAKE

Flatten a sheet of junk clay to ⅛″ thick. Cover the armature with this sheet, smudging seams to blend edges. Form head into a thick spoon shape, leaving neck very thin. Smooth the front surface by rolling between your palms. Check the body from all angles. Bake the armature for thirty minutes. Cool.

STEP 3 SCULPTING A HEAD

Form head shape the same as you did for William. Use a needle tool to mark the halfway line on the front of the face. Since Randy is quite young, his eyes are lower on his head than his parents' eyes. Use a round tool to center each eye socket right on the halfway line. Now mark the face into thirds. Draw in the eyebrows. Draw the nose on the bottom line. Divide the lower third into thirds and draw in the mouth.

Check Randy's profile. Is it rounded like an egg? Is the back of his neck high enough?

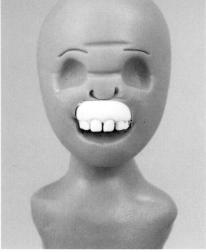

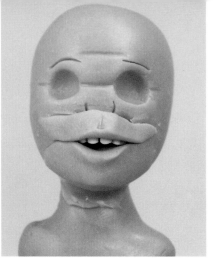

STEP 4 TEETH

To make teeth for Randy, wrap foil around a wooden dowel. Lay a strip of white clay around the dowel. Use the fingernail tool, described in chapter two, to mark in teeth. Keep them even. Bake teeth on dowel.

Use a large needle tool to press in a mouth. Roll the tool to smooth the interior edges. Trim back edge of teeth. Place baked teeth over the upper edge of mouth. Looks ghoulish, doesn't it?

You will be adding a lip piece over the teeth. Will the current teeth position make the lips stick out too far? If so, push teeth deeper. Make all of the add-on facial features the same as you did for William and Margaret. Try each on for size. Lay lips over teeth, then proceed just as you did for his parents' faces.

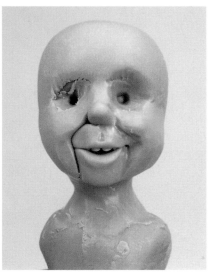

◄ STEP 5 CHEEKS

Notice that Randy's cheeks are chubbier than his parents' cheeks.

▶ As I blended in the cheeks, I decided to cut away some of the fat. He was too puffy. Remember: As you practice, all of this cutting and adding and blending will get easier and easier. You can do it.

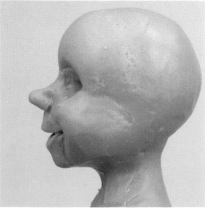

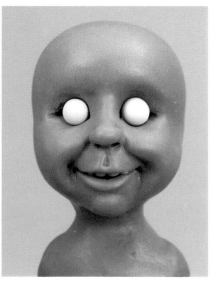

Check the profile. Some questions to ask are: Does he still look like a kid? Have the eyes stayed on the halfway line? Is his nose too big? Is the chin too strong for a child?

His eyes seem large in his face, but this is OK if you want to emphasize his innocence. Continue to smooth and refine the surface.

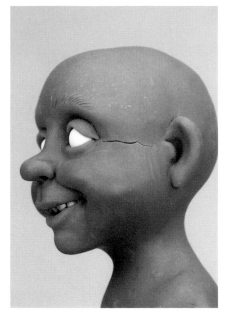
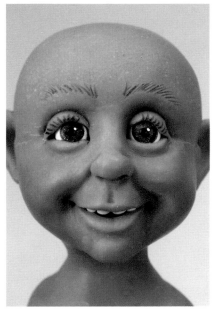
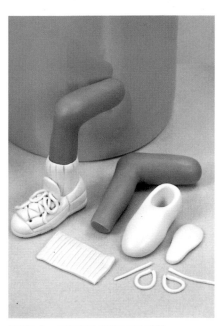

STEP 6 THE SECOND BAKE

Add ears and eyelids. Draw in eyebrows with the needle tool. Add blush. Bake head and body. Cool. Notice that a small crack appeared during baking. These cracks most frequently appear near the eyes, where the clay has been compressed. They are an un-predictable nuisance, but one that can be mostly solved with refilling and rebaking. Sometimes I add freckles to help camou-flage the cracks.

STEP 7 PAINTING THE EYES

Paint the eyes the same as you did for Sweet Suzette (page 36), except make them brown.

STEP 8 SHOES AND SOCKS

Make his legs from 2″ × ½″ ropes. Taper and press into a leg shape with knee and calf. (See chapter five, Sweet Suzette.) Each shoe begins with a ¾″ white ball pressed into a shoe shape. Use the dowel to hollow a space for the ankle. For sock, mark rib-bing lines into a ½″-wide strip and wrap around ankle. Stick ankle into shoe. Add tongue, stitch marks, tread and shoestrings. (See Studious Stan's shoes in chapter five if you need help.)

STEP 9 SHORTS

To make shorts, begin with a flattened pan-cake, just like those used in chapter five. Press pancake over bottom of body. For pant legs, roll two 1″ balls into 1¼″ ropes. Hollow the center of each. Flatten the inside top thigh and blend firmly into pants bot-tom. Set Randy on a foil-covered square-edged baking pan. Press legs in place.

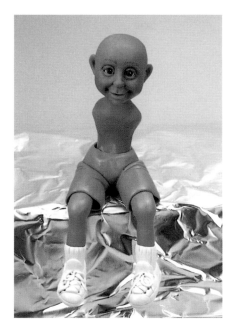

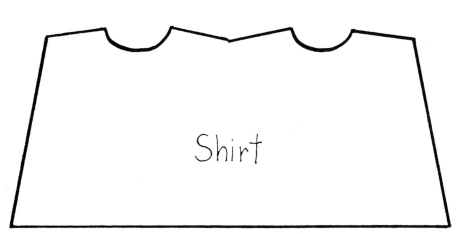

Pattern for Randy's shirt.

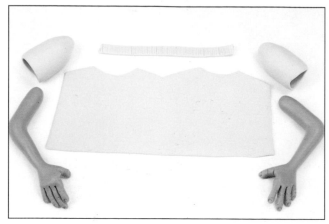

For Randy's shirt, using the pattern given, cut the first pieces from a sheet of flattened clay. Press with fabric for texture. For sleeve, roll two ½″ × 1″ ropes. Hollow the centers. Make arms following directions in chapter four. His arms are 2½″ from fingertip to top, with the hand being 1″ long.

Join the short ends of the shirt to form a tube. Slip shirt over Randy's head. Place arms into sleeves, then add them simultaneously by pressing them against the body from opposite sides. Press shoulders with fabric to erase fingerprints. Add neck trim.

STEP 10   HAIR

For hair, fringe the long edge of a 2″-wide black clay strip. To form a base for the hair, press a ¾″ black clay ball firmly over the top of his head. Add a few pieces of hair at a time, ending with the center spot on top of his head.

Place partially baked dog under Randy's arm (see page 79 for steps to make the dog). Push it firmly against his body so that he and the dog will bake as one piece.

STEP 11   THE THIRD BAKE

Position Randy's hand so that he can hold a fishing pole. Bake for thirty minutes. Cool in oven.

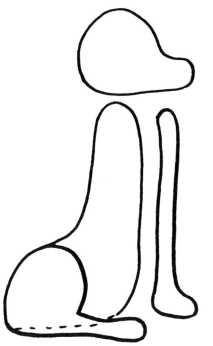

Pattern for Mutt Lee.

Mutt Lee

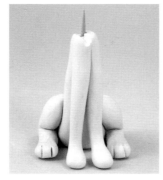

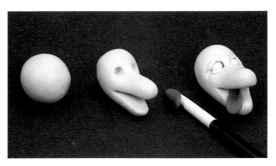

STEP 1   BODY

Roll a 1½" ball of white clay into a cone shape. Curve cone so that it fits the pattern. Insert a sturdy toothpick into the body. Make four leg shapes, following patterns. Press against body. Mark in toenails.

STEP 2   HEAD

Roll a ⅞"-diameter white ball into a teardrop shape. On the small end, cut in the mouth. Press in holes for eyes. For the tongue, press a small, flattened pink teardrop onto the end of a brush handle. Press into mouth, rolling brush to loosen and position tongue. Press in pre-baked eyes.

STEP 3   THE FIRST BAKE

Place the head onto the end of the toothpick. Set dog on baking sheet. Prop head between two ceramic coffee mugs to keep his body from tipping over in the oven. Bake for thirty minutes. Cool.

Flatten a sheet of very soft white clay, such as Sculpey III or FIMO Soft. Wrap around the dog's body.

Completely cover dog's body with this soft clay. Clean clay from around eyes and mouth.

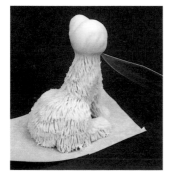

STEP 4   FUR

Cut in hair marks over entire body. Set him on a piece of paper to turn him without touching the soft body. His nose is a black clay ball.

For ears and tail, place warm, soft clay into a garlic press or clay gun. Press out tiny ropes. Remove ropes from disk with needle tool and roll against head to loosen and attach.

Press out longer pieces to use as the tail. Add fluff over the eyes. Tuck Mutt Lee under Randy's arm, as described previously. (If you want to make Mutt Lee by himself, prop him as you did for the first bake and bake according to the manufacturer's instructions for the brand of soft clay you used.)

CHAPTER SEVEN

The Family Reunion: Creating Expressive Figures

Bring creative expression to your characters by giving them the ability to stand on their own two feet and to gesture emphatically with their hands. After all, who ever saw a family reunion where everyone sat meekly still with their arms crossed in their laps? Real people mingle and relate. In this chapter, I'll show you how to use a wire armature that will allow your characters to do just that.

I'll also show you how to create patterns for clothing so you will have more freedom in dressing your people. A few general principles will allow you to design unique outfits that will fit the bodies and moods of your people. The last section, on millefiori, which is the art of layering colored clay to create a design, will allow you to create intricately patterned clothing and accessories. (The checkerboard and Grandpa's vest on the opposite page were done in this manner—no, that's not paint!) Imagine this chapter to be like a costume shop where you can mix and match which clothes to put on which character.

If, at this point, you are feeling overwhelmed by all of the new things that you are learning, skip the patterned clothing for your own characters and make the clothes in plain col-

ors. They'll still be terrific! I just have so much fun with the millefiori clothing that I wanted to be sure and introduce you to the possibilities in this technique.

PLANNING YOUR COLOR PALETTE

If you like to experiment with different color combinations and patterns and allow them to inspire your figure's character, then the first thing you need to do is gather together your palette of clay colors. Lay balls and ropes of color next to each other on the table, then stand back, squint your eyes a little and see if anything clashes. Play around with mixing some of the colors together, as we did in chapter six, to see if that will make them more harmonious. Lighten some colors by adding a pastel, white or beige. If you want to make some millefiori canes to create patterned clothing, now is the time. Refer to page 99 for directions.

WHAT YOU'LL NEED FOR THESE PROJECTS:
- Polymer clay in your choice of brands and colors
- A selection of prebaked white-clay eyeballs ⅛″ to ¼″ in diameter
- Acrylic paint:
  - blue
  - black
  - brown
  - white
  - blush tone
- Pink makeup blush or chalk
- 14-gauge wire (heavy clothes-hanger wire)
- Fine wire for earrings (optional)
- Green floral wire for flowers (optional)
- Small wicker basket (optional)
- Aluminum foil
- Knife
- Rolling pin or pasta machine
- Assorted brushes (no. 2 and or no. 4 filbert, no. 3 round, no. 1 liner)
- Oven
- Oven thermometer
- Round-nose pliers
- Wire cutters
- Needle tools (both sharp and blunt)
- Fingernail tool
- Ruler
- Fabric for textures

I chose this palette of plain colors and patterned millefiori canes when I began working on the Family Reunion people.

PLANNING YOUR CHARACTERS

If creating specific characters is the most important aspect of figure making for you, then your first task is to choose what characters you are going to make. Will they be male or female? Skinny or fat? Old or young? Will they be standing or sitting? How will you pose their arms?

Once you have decided which character to make, draw a rough stick-figure sketch of its height and position of arms and legs. This will be the guide you will refer to as you decide how big the head will be and how long to make the arms and legs. Since these are caricatures, you can use your own judgment as to body proportions. A cartoon-like style works fine for these little people. But if you want more help with realistic proportions, refer to a good drawing anatomy book, such as my three favorites, which are listed in the Resources section.

MAKING THE ARMATURES

Once you know how tall, how fat and in what position your characters will be, then you are ready to make the armatures. These armatures are very similar to those used for The People Next Door, but they have an additional wire to support either the legs or arms. You could also make one character who has a wire to support both legs and arms.

I usually wrap foil around the wire armature to give it bulk, then cover the foil with a layer of clay. If the character is very skinny, eliminate the foil and just use clay over the wires. The shape of the armature is critical, as it really does determine the body image of your character. If your person has a potbelly or sagging bosom, that needs to be there in the armature. If you envision a delicate little child, then the armature will need to be really thin so that the addition of the layers of skin and clothing don't end up making it too bulky.

The following pictures show the actual armatures that are inside each of the Family Reunion people.

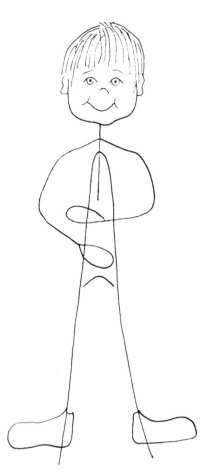

This is the sketch I drew of the little boy cousin when I began planning the characters for the family reunion.

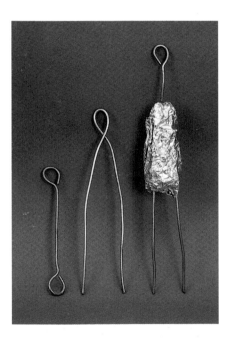

◄ For the standing characters, cut two wires. Measure the longest one so that it will fit from the base of one foot, up to the shoulders, loop and go back down to the other heel. Refer to your sketch to make sure your lengths are right. When measuring this wire, be sure to add an extra ⅓″ to protrude through the bottom of each heel. This will go into the base support. Wrap foil around the middle of this bent wire to form the trunk of the body. Embed the shorter wire into the middle of the foil to support the head.

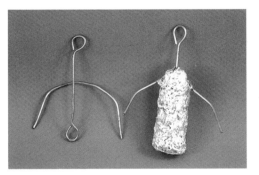

For sitting characters with extended arms, cut one wire to embed into the center of the foil to support the head and neck. Cut a second wire that is the combined length of your character's two arms, plus a little extra for the body width. Put this through the shoulder area and wrap it securely with foil to hold it in place. Don't worry about the bend of the arms. You can change the arms later.

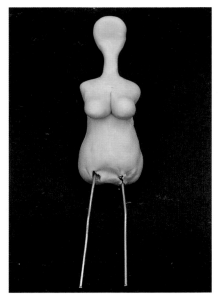

Grandma Bethal Grace and her armature.

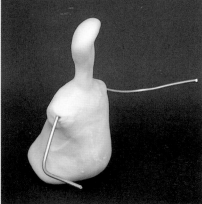

Grandpa Roy Arlie and his armature.

Aunt Phyllis Rose and her armature.

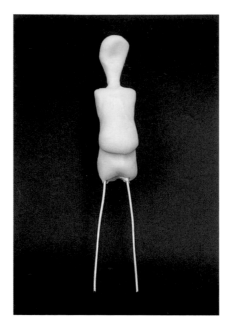

Uncle Matthew Kent and his armature.

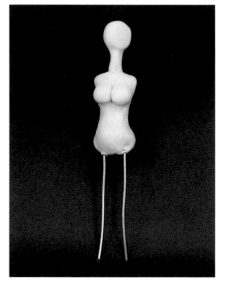

Cousin Ellie Sean and her armature.

Cousin Bryce Scott and his armature.

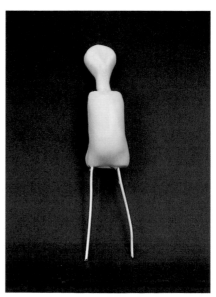

Sculpting the Heads

To make each of these heads, I used the basic sculpting procedure demonstrated in chapter six. When checking your own sculpting, remember that all facial features need to be visible from a profile view, because the face is round, not square. Even though all characters start the same, each has its own unique look due to the size and position of the features.

After the head is completely sculpted and blushed for color, bake it for approximately twenty minutes. The flesh tones will gradually darken each time they are baked, so I suggest a shorter time on these initial bakings. After the head is cooled, paint the eyes and eyebrows, following directions on pages 26 and 27.

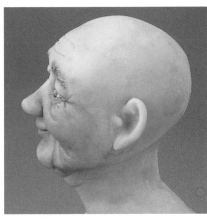

◄ Notice that Grandma's mouth is quite close to her nose. She must be having dental problems. Her wrinkles are quite pronounced. The third eyelid piece droops slightly over her upper lids.

► Can you tell I'm partial to large noses? I think that Grandpa's gives him a commanding presence. His type of face is my favorite to sculpt—and one of the easiest.

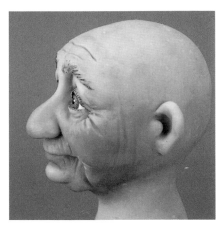

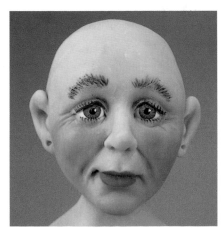

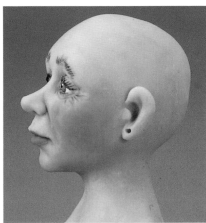

◄ Aunt Phyllis Rose is the cynical one in the family. Notice how her mouth curls up on the left side. She has holes in her ears so that I can insert earrings later. Compare the bridge of her nose with Grandma's and Grandpa's.

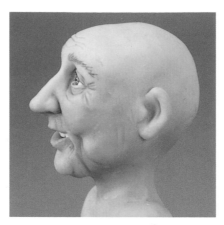

◄ Uncle Matthew Kent's face is longer and thinner than the rest, and there is very little dip in the bridge of his nose. Compare the profile of his lips to Auntie's.

Cousin Ellie Sean has a heart-shaped face with few wrinkles. Notice the upward tilt of her nose, which is small compared with Auntie's.

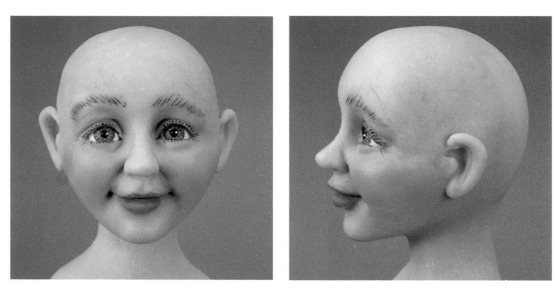

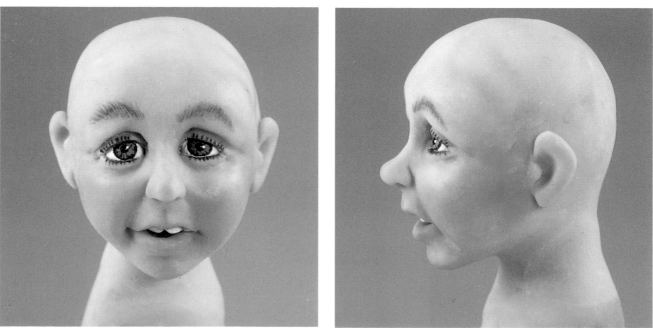

Cousin Bryce Scott didn't really want to come to this reunion. You can tell by the downward tilt of his mouth that he is not too sure about the whole thing. Notice how his cheeks still look like baby cheeks in their fullness near the chin.

Adding Legs and Bases

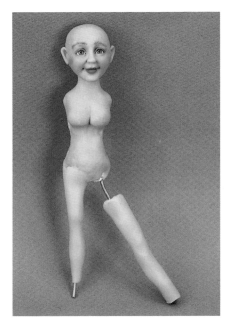

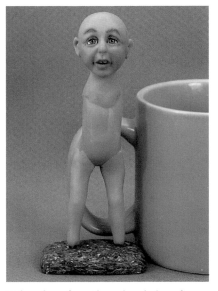

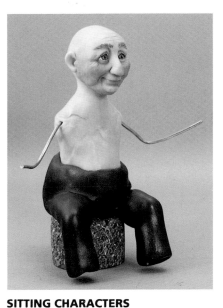

STANDING CHARACTERS

Roll a tube of flesh clay the approximate size you need for your character's leg. Shape it slightly by tapering toward the ankle and rolling a bulge at the calf and knee. Use a sharp needle tool to make a hole part way through the leg, then thread it onto the wire. Be sure to leave some wire exposed. Blend the thighs into the body slightly. Stretch and roll the leg to get rid of cellulite and lumps.

Make a base from the colored clay of your choice. I used leftover chunks of various greens, golds and blues, which I chopped in the food processor until they looked like linoleum. Then I patted them into various shapes to serve as bases for each character. Until the base is baked, it is not sturdy enough to support the figure, so lean the character against a stable surface while you are preparing the shoes.

SITTING CHARACTERS

Grandpa's legs are exactly like those in chapter five and six—made with a flat pancake shape put on first to cover the bottom. Then two partially hollowed tubes are blended on for the pant legs. Grandpa's are hollowed to the knee. The stool is made in the same way as the bases for the standing characters.

SHOES

The general guideline for determining the size of the shoe is to make it slightly longer than the length of the head. (Take your own shoe and look into the mirror with it next to your face.) Because my characters have heads that are larger than average, and legs that are shorter than average, I decided to go with slightly smaller shoes that would better match their legs. You decide what looks best on your characters.

To give support to the shoes and ankles for sitting characters, a toothpick is embedded into the center of each leg. Then the leg is inserted into the hollow pant leg.

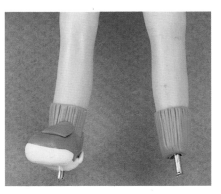

When putting the socks and shoes over the legs of the standing characters, be sure to leave the wire protruding through the bottom of the shoe, so that it can be reattached to the base.

A Gallery of Shoes

To get ideas for shoes, look into your closet and actually copy the piecing and stitch marks in some of your own shoes. That's what I did for these. If you need help figuring out how to make these shoes, refer to chapter five.

Once the shoes are on, it is time to bake again—for twenty minutes. Be sure to prop each of the characters so that they don't tip over in the oven. They may feel very stable once the shoes are on, but don't let that fool you. Once they are hot, they *will* tip. Ceramic coffee mugs are my favorite props.

Creating a Pattern for Pants

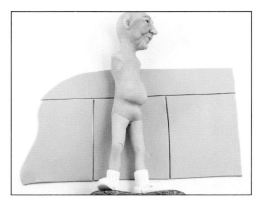

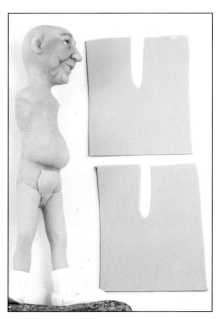

Place a strip of raw clay over the character's crotch to serve as a base to attach the pants to. Cut a narrow strip out of the middle top of each pants piece. This opening should reach from the character's waist to the center crotch (this section will be the inseam of the pants leg).

To make pants, roll out a ³⁄₁₆″-thick sheet of clay. I use the no. 4 setting on my pasta machine. Lay the character on top of the clay and cut a width that will fit from waist to pant leg hem. Now cut two pieces that are each wide enough to wrap from the character's center back to its center front. It is better at this point to cut it too big rather than too small. Press the clay with fabric to give it texture.

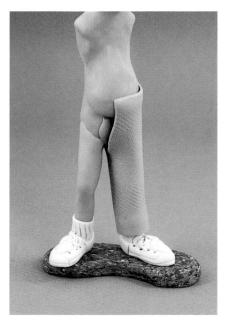

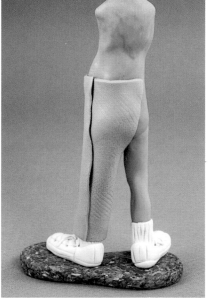

Fit one piece between the character's legs, then wrap the piece around the leg and body so that the seam overlaps on the side. If it doesn't fit the first time, just try again—nothing is wasted except a little practice time. This is easier than sewing with needle and thread, isn't it? If it doesn't quite fit, just stretch it a little.

Add the second piece exactly like the first, being sure that the pieces overlap in the crotch area.

Creating a Pattern for Shorts

Shorts are put on exactly like long pants—except for their shorter legs. The women with skirts also have shorts like these, as I feel funny leaving them without any underwear!

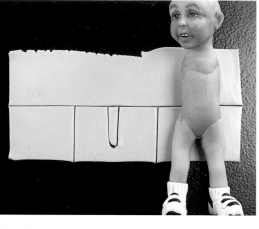

Roll out a sheet of clay and cut two pieces wide enough to wrap from center back to center front.

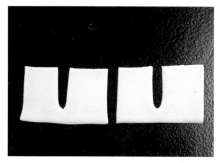

Cut a notch in the middle top of each piece.

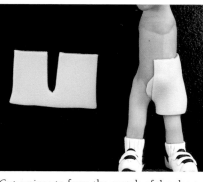

Cut a piece to form the crotch of the shorts. Wrap the first piece around one of the character's legs.

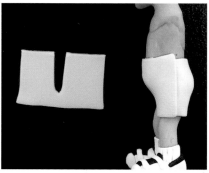

Join the seams at the character's side.

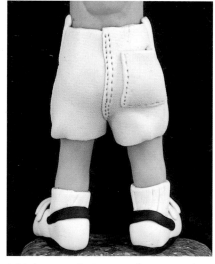

Add the second piece, overlapping at the crotch. Add a small square for a pocket. Use a needle tool to press in stitch lines at the seams and around the pocket.

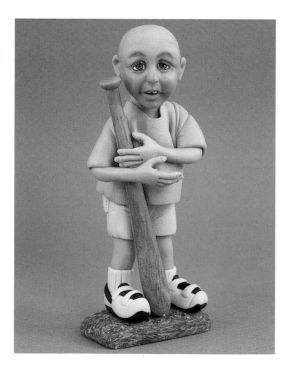

Bryce has a much simpler shirt than Uncle Matthew, but it was measured and put on in the same way as shown on page 91.

Creating a Shirt Pattern

Lay the character on top of a rolled-out sheet of clay. Cut a piece that is wide enough to fit from the top of the shoulder to the bottom of the shirt. Uncle's shirt is going to look as though it were tucked in, so I cut it at the waistband. Now cut it long enough to fit around his whole body. Not sure how long? Just make a quick guess. You can always do it again.

Shape the shirt pieces by angling the top to fit over the shoulders. Cut out a semicircle at the front and back neck area. For Uncle's shirt, I cut a collar piece and two cuffs. I also cut a slit in the center front where I will later add buttons.

▶ To measure the length of the arm, temporarily attach the tube sleeve to the character's shoulder. Most adult wrists reach to the thigh. Cut the sleeve at that point. You can always trim off more later.

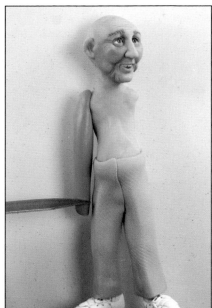

For extra support, press a wad of raw clay over the shoulder area, just as you did in chapters five and six. Lay the back of the shirt on first, then the front, with the shoulders overlapping. Now cut a length of the pants color to use as a belt or waistband.

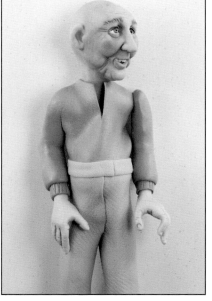

Wrap the waistband in place. Press with fabric to give texture and a smooth fit. Add arms and sleeves. How big should the hands be? For an average adult, measured from fingertip to wrist, they are two-thirds the length of the head.

Fit sleeves so they look rounded at the shoulder area. There is supposed to be an arm in there, so don't let it look flat. Press with fabric for texture and add wrinkles with a blunt-edged tool. Press in button-holes. Add the collar and tiny balls for buttons. Notice that I put a ribbed texture on both the collar and the cuffs.

Adding Arms Over a Wire Armature

I personally dislike the tediousness of adding arms over a wire armature, but the wire does allow you to support the arms in a way that is nearly impossible with just clay. So sometimes it's worth doing it. The problem is that the wire keeps poking through just when you have it about right. So, now that I've given that warning and you've gritted your teeth, are you ready to try this?

Bend the wire so that the elbows and wrists are in the position you have planned. Notice that Grandpa's wrist wire is bent slightly because I plan on having his hands drop down a bit. Make the hands and the tubes for the sleeves. Don't hollow out the sleeves. Use a needle tool to puncture a hole through the center of the sleeve and into each wrist. Thread the sleeves onto the wires. Sometimes it is easier to get them on if you cut each sleeve at the elbow, then blend the seam after the sleeve is on.

Once the sleeves are blended and shaped, press them with fabric for texture. Thread the hand over the wire. Be sure that the wrist and hand are in the position that you have chosen. One way that I judge positioning is to pretend that I am the character and then look at my own wrist to see what the angles are and where the skin wrinkles.

Add cuff pieces to cover up the seam where the wrist and sleeve join.

◄ Cut a piece for the shirt back and one for each side of the front. To determine the exact size, measure length and width the same as you did for Uncle Matthew's shirt.

Softly turn under the bottom edges of all shirt pieces, then position them. Overlap one front piece over the other, just like with a real shirt.

Add the collar and buttons. Use a fine-tipped needle tool to punch holes in the buttons. Use a brush to tuck in and position the shirt.

Making a Vest

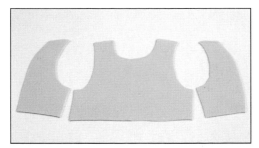

If you wish to make a patterned vest, refer to page 99 for instructions on how to create a millefiori loaf. Use a very sharp blade, such as a wallpaper scraper replacement blade

Grandpa's vest has a millefiori pattern on it, but you can make yours plain if you aren't ready to try millefiori yet. Cut pieces similar to those in the picture, measuring the same as you would for a shirt, except the vest doesn't have to really fit over his belly. (I know that several of my own would never successfully close in the front!)

or a tissue blade, to cut thin slices from the millefiori loaf or cane. Lay these slices over the surface of the vest pieces. Attaching the end of the millefiori loaf to a block of raw clay makes it easier to hold and allows you to slice all the way to the end of the loaf without fear of cutting your fingers.

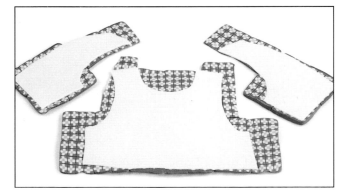

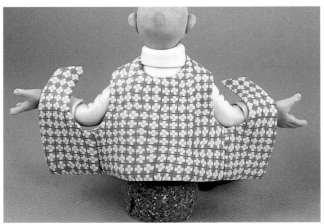

Lay the vest onto a piece of fabric. This will prevent it from sticking to the table, plus it will give it texture. Roll and press the side of your hand over the surface to blend the seams between the millefiori squares. Don't roll the vest through the pasta machine, as it will distort the pattern. Trim the edges.

Overlap the side seams, then fit the vest onto the character.

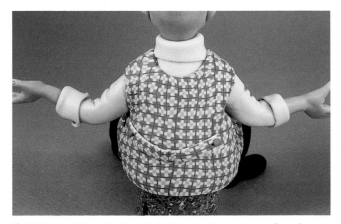

If desired, add a strip for a belt. Press a button on each end.

Position the front. Add buttonholes and buttons.

Measuring and Fitting a Dress

Lay character over a rolled-out sheet of clay. Cut a width that will fit at least once around the body. Angle the sides so the dress will be narrower at the top than at the bottom. Cut length so it will fit from the top of the shoulders to the desired hemline.

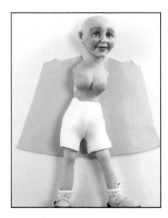

This dress is designed to seam at the center back. Lay character over pattern and mark the neckline. Cut a semicircle at the center neckline. Angle the shoulders and cut a quarter circle at each top outside edge. This edge will be the back neckline when it is seamed. Cut the hemline at a slight curve.

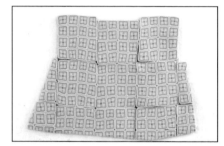

If you wish the dress to have a printed design, cut millefiori squares and lay over the surface of the dress. You can also leave it plain. I usually lay the pieces on a piece of fabric to keep them from sticking to the table as I work.

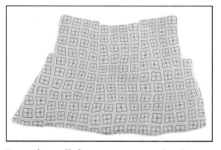

Press the millefiori squares together by pressing and rolling with the palm of your hand or a rolling pin.

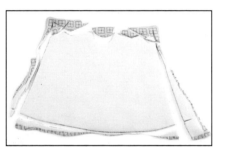

Trim the edges.

Pick up the dress and form it into a tube shape by overlapping the back seam. Slip the dress over the figure's head. Fit the dress to the character's body by readjusting and trimming the back seam.

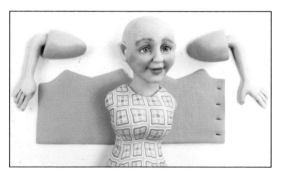

For a simple dress, sleeves can now be added in the same way you added sleeves to shirts in chapter five. Instead of adding sleeves, I decided to give this character a short jacket. That way I wouldn't have to match the pattern on the sleeves and bodice. The arms are slipped into a hollowed sleeve shape. The jacket is cut the same as for a short shirt.

Position sleeves and press in place. Be sure that the tops of the sleeves look rounded, then add texture. Add buttonholes and buttons.

Making a Skirt

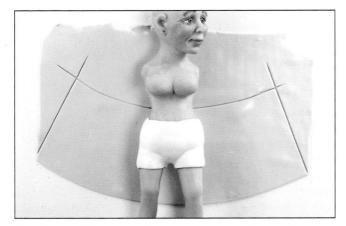

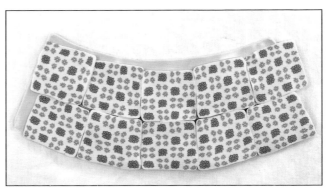

To make the skirt, lay the character over a sheet of clay. Cut a piece approximately three times as wide as the character and as long as you wish the finished skirt to be. Notice that the piece is cut on a curve so that the top is narrower than the bottom. This will keep the waist from looking quite so bunchy. Aunt Phyllis already has short, thick little legs; she doesn't need a fat tummy, too.

If you wish a printed fabric, lay the millefiori slices over the skirt and press to join all seams.

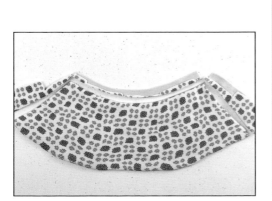

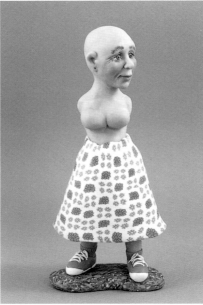

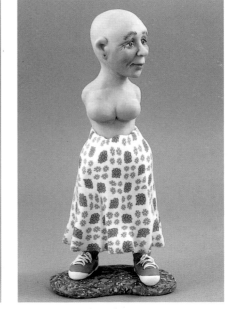

Press with fabric for texture, then trim seams.

Join the short ends of the skirt to create a tube and slip over the character's head. Press in gathers at waist to fit skirt.

Gently scrunch the bottom of the skirt to create soft, natural folds.

Making a Blouse and Jacket

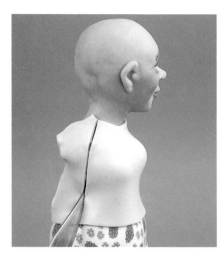

If you wish the blouse fabric to be patterned, add millefiori pieces. Press with fabric for texture. Trim edges.

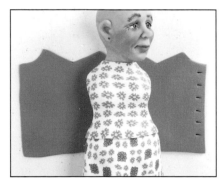

Cut a jacket piece using the same techniques as for a shirt.

To make the blouse front, cut a shirt front from a sheet of clay, measuring it the same as you did the shirt for Uncle Matthew. Stretch the front over the character's bodice and trim side seams.

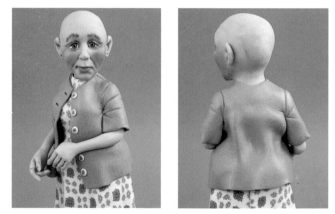

Add sleeves, arms, buttons and buttonholes the same as you did for Cousin Ellie. Note that Aunt Phyllis's jacket is longer to cover her spreading middle. I recognize the attempt to cover!

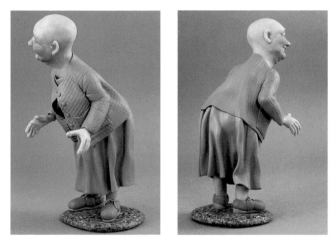

Grandma's outfit is made exactly like Auntie's, except the skirt is fuller and her sleeves are longer.

Designing Hats

The last thing to add to your character is the hair and, if desired, a hat. The hair can be any of the styles demonstrated in previous chapters in this book. The proper hat is a finishing touch that adds special personality. If doing caricatures of real people, hats are also great for giving a clue to someone's interests or hobbies. Most hats can be made as a variation of one of the following styles.

A floppy newsboy-style hat works well as a golf hat or a captain's hat.

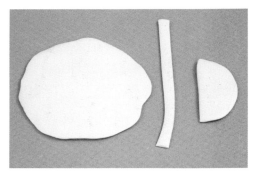

From a flattened sheet, cut a circle that is almost twice as wide as the top of the head. The long strip should go three-fifths of the way around the head. The flat bill shape is as wide as the head.

Fit the strip around the head, then lay the bill over the front. Complete the hat by turning a soft hem all the way around the large circle, then just press this circle over the head.

A baseball cap.

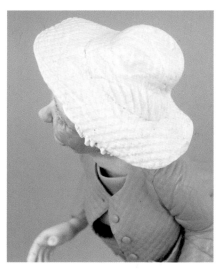

A floppy straw hat.

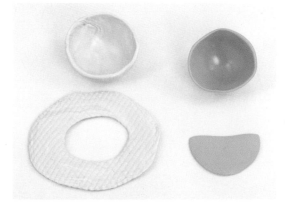

Both of these hats are composed of two pieces. For the straw hat, cut a circle one and a half times as wide as the head from flattened clay. Cut the center out of the circle. For the tops of both hats, roll a ball that is about one-third the size of the head. Hollow out the center with a rounded tool like a blunt handle or dowel.

Set the crowns on top of the bottom pieces and press the edges together by pressing your thumb or finger inside the hat. Add texture by pressing with a piece of fabric. Mark stitch lines into the baseball hat and add a tiny flattened ball at the center point. Add flowers, ribbons, bows or feathers to the straw hat, if desired.

Accessories

Taking the time to add an accessory to your character's hands will make its story come alive. This little person is now doing something we can relate to. The extra effort is well worth it in terms of emotional response from viewers—or from recipients of a special gift that includes their favorite sport or hobby.

GOLF CLUB

The golf club is a straight stick, such as a bamboo skewer, that is cut to the desired length. One end is wrapped with a piece of black clay, then scored with a knife to resemble wrapped tape. For the other end, shape a piece of black clay into the wedge shape of a golf club head. Add some silver clay (ProMat and Sculpey III both come in a terrific silver color) trim to the flat side of the club. Press the head onto the handle, then bake. After baking, paint the handle with silver paint or a silver wax finish such as Rub'n Buff.

BASEBALL BAT AND BALL

To keep the bat straight, a wire, such as a piece of clothes-hanger wire, is embedded into the center of a brown clay rope. If you wish the clay to have stripes like the grain of wood, mix several colors of brown together, leaving the clay partially mixed. Roll and stretch the clay to taper it toward the small end. Press a flattened clay ball to the small end for the guard. For the baseball, roll a small, round ball. Use a needle tool to draw in the stitch lines. Bake both bat and ball. After cooling, stain both with black acrylic paint, brushing it on and then immediately wiping it off.

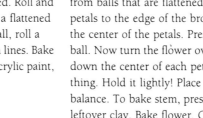

FLOWERS

This flower stem begins the same as Margaret Joyce's (page 74). First, make the leaves and wrap the stem end of each leaf around a green florist wire.

To make the blossom, start with a small brown ball. Form petals from balls that are flattened and shaped with your fingers. Press petals to the edge of the brown ball. Add a small green ball over the center of the petals. Press a hole into the center of this green ball. Now turn the flower over and use a needle tool to draw a line down the center of each petal. Be careful not to flatten the whole thing. Hold it lightly! Place blossom onto stem to see if it will balance. To bake stem, press it into a holder made from a piece of leftover clay. Bake flower. Cool. Use superglue to attach blossom securely to stem.

CHECKERBOARD

Make a black-and-white millefiori checkerboard following the directions on the next page. You will need four slices with sixteen squares in each slice. For the base, from a flattened brown sheet cut a square that is slightly larger than the width of two checkerboard slices laid side by side.

Lay the checkerboard squares onto the base. Press to join the seams. Keep sides square. Cut small strips to frame the board. Lay them in place. To make the brown clay resemble wood, use a needle tool to draw in grain lines and tiny holes.

To make checkers, from flattened black and red clay sheets use a 3/16" Kemper pattern cutter to make twelve circles of each color. If you don't have a cutter, you can just roll and flatten tiny balls. Press the checkers onto the unbaked board. Bake for thirty minutes.

Millefiori

All of the patterns in these clay loaves are created by layering thin sheets or ropes of colored clay. There is no paint used in this process. The technique is an ancient one originally used with glass and ceramic clays. You may have also seen it done with layers of colored candy to make those colorful old-fashioned Christmas candies, or with colored waxes to make elegant candles.

The name comes from the Italian *mille*, meaning thousand, and *fiori*, meaning flowers. Translated, this means a thousand flowers, which is what you might get if you slice one of the flower canes.

The trick to the whole process is to start very large, and then stretch and reduce the diameter of the cane (if it is round) or loaf (if it is square) so that the image appears smaller. It is also important to have a very sharp blade to use for slicing, so that the design is not distorted by the drag of the blade. The easiest such blade to find is a wallpaper scraper replacement blade from the wallpaper department at your local hardware store.

Once you have made millefiori canes, you can save leftovers for six months or more to use in other projects. These little bits and pieces of canes become like a treasure hoard.

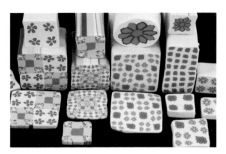

Several clay manufacturers produce ready-made clay millefiori canes that may be used for your project. If using these ready-made canes, be sure to warm them before attempting to manipulate them, as they may be somewhat brittle from sitting in the package for a while.

Checkerboard

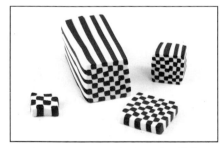

Let's begin with a checkerboard millefiori because it is one of the easiest to make. It is also one of the most impressive—when all of the lines come together just right. It does take a little practice, so you might want to begin by using a favorite color—blue for example—and white, so that if you make lots of mistakes you will just end up with a terrific pile of marbled blue! You could then use this for other projects. There are several other ways to make a checkerboard, but this is my favorite.

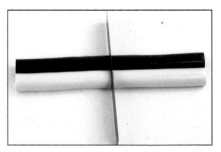

Roll two 6″ ropes of contrasting colors. Be sure that they are as close as possible to the same size. Flatten the top slightly by rolling across it twice with a brayer or rolling pin. Cut the ropes into two equal pieces.

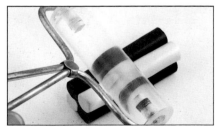

Stack the resulting four pieces so that you have a checkerboard design. Be sure that both ends match and that all of the ropes are aligned. Make each side square by rolling across it with the brayer or a rolling pin. Keep rolling and turning, rolling and turning, until the loaf starts to elongate. You can alternate this rolling with pressing on the loaf with the flat of your hand.

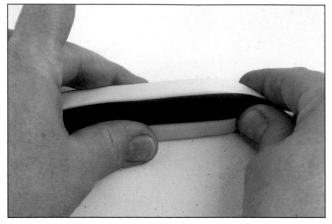

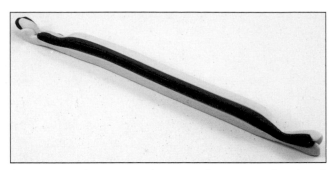

Grasp a little bit of clay at one end of the loaf and, with the other hand, stretch gently but firmly as you slide your fingers along the sides. It is important to keep uniform pressure on your fingers as you slide them so that the diameter of the loaf stays uniform.

Concentrate on keeping your fingers steady. Now switch ends and stretch in the opposite direction. Keep doing this, switching ends frequently, until the loaf is 12″ long.

Stack the four pieces to make a 16-square checkerboard. Be sure that both ends are aligned.

Trim off the ends that have become distorted. Cut the remaining loaf into four equal parts. If there are any extra-thick or extra-thin sections, discard them, as they will wreck the checkerboard effect.

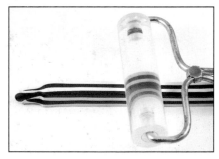

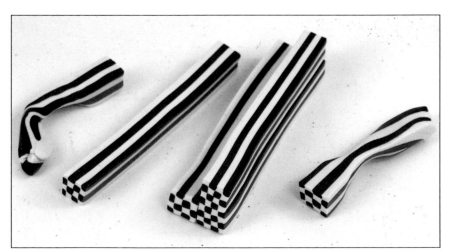

Repeat the rolling and stretching process until the loaf is again 12″ long.

Trim away the ends and cut the remaining uniform loaf into 4 equal pieces. Stack so that you now have sixty-four squares in the loaf. Be sure that both ends are aligned. You can reduce it more if you like, but I usually stop at this point.

9-Patch Quilt Squares

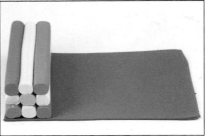

This 9-patch looks complicated, but it was made just like the checkerboard, except that nine ropes were used in the first step and a thin blanket was wrapped around the loaf.

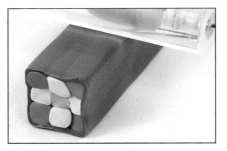

◄ The loaf is then pressed, rolled and stretched to reduce its size.

► The resulting long loaf is cut into four equal parts and then reassembled.

When the loaf is reduced again and then reassembled, the original thin blanket wrap makes the design look like a plaid. Notice how the colors seem to change as the design gets smaller. One of the most important aspects of this type of a design is your choice of color. Be sure that you have high contrast between colors, or the design will get lost.

At first glance, these may look like totally different designs, but they both began exactly like the original 9-patch, except that the small logs were each wrapped individually. The large square on the left was built without using an outer blanket wrap. The large square on the right was built with a 9-patch that had three wraps around the original loaf (magenta, white and green), which is shown here on top of the large square.

Flowers

All of these flowers are made with the techniques that follow. The variety comes from the decision to wrap or not wrap the individual ropes and from the choice of colors.

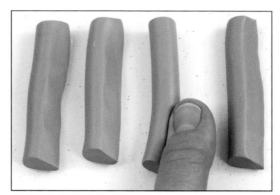

For a flower with five petals, roll a colored rope that is 10″ long. Cut into five equal parts. Flatten one side of each rope. Repeat with a contrasting color.

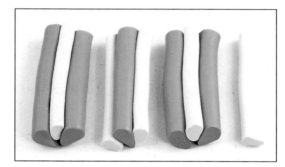

Stack the contrasting ropes like little submarine sandwiches, with the darker color on the outside of two sandwiches, and the light color on the outside of one. You will have one light piece left over.

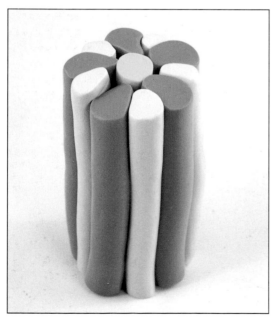

Roll a center that is 2″ long. Stack the sandwiches around the center, adding the extra light piece so that no color is next to a rope of like color. Be sure that both ends are aligned.

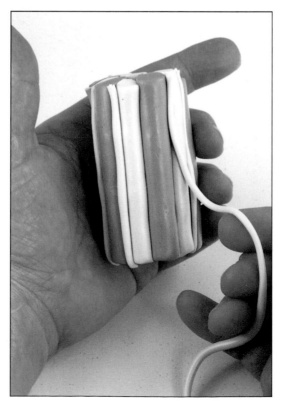

Your goal is to end up with a cane that is round on the outside edge and that has very few air holes through the center. To accomplish this, add tiny ropes along the outside edge to fill in any gaps. Hold the cane lightly so that you don't distort it while you are working.

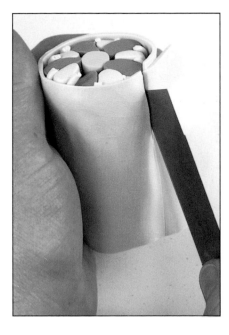

◄ Cut a thin blanket that fits around the cane with no overlap. Trim the ends so that they meet but don't overlap.

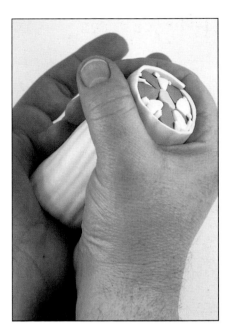

► Squeeze the cane firmly along its length to compact the ropes. I know this is painful after all of that work, but it is necessary. If the inside ropes don't stick together, you are apt to end up with an airspace that will distort the whole design.

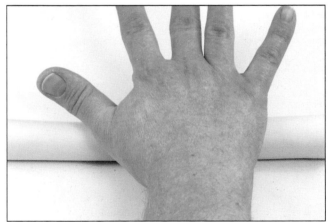

◄ Roll and stretch the cane. I often use my palm when rolling so I don't get dips that are caused by uneven finger pressure. Frequently pick up the rope with both hands and pull firmly, but slowly, to stretch it.

When the cane is the desired diameter, stop and cut it with a sharp blade. (Your flower may not be perfect, but it looks like a flower, doesn't it? It will look better as you reduce its size.) You can use the cane as it is or recombine it with others to create a new design.

This shows the process of making round canes into a square loaf. Squares work better when making fabric for characters' clothes, as the edges will match—circles always leave gaps. This loaf was reduced and combined by the same process as the checkerboard loaves.

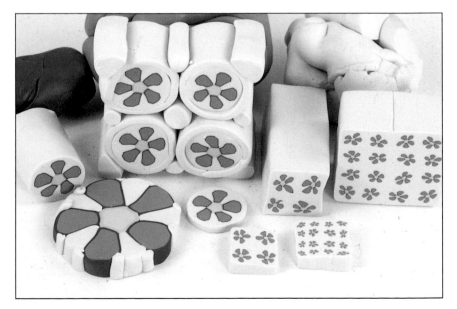

CHAPTER EIGHT

Special Visitors: Saving Time With Shortcuts

Fantasy characters may just be my favorite ones to make, for with fantasy, one's imagination is invited to be outrageously present. For instance, we all know that a real person couldn't fit into a teacup, but a leprechaun could and should—and would. Now, with the skills that you have learned in this book—and with the marvelously lifelike qualities of polymer clay—you can make your fantasies come to life. Put that little fellow in the teacup, along with his bathwater and his rubber ducky. Makes you smile, doesn't it, to see this world that you've created from just a lump of clay?

In this chapter, besides encouraging you to play with your imagination, I will also show you three shortcuts for creating characters. We don't always have to do things the hard way, despite the lessons that Grandma drilled into our childhood heads about hard work and perseverance building character and paying big dividends in the long run. That's true, but take some shortcuts and use the saved time to create some wonderful accessory pieces, like St. Nick's marionette.

USING PUSH MOLDS

Yes, push molds do work for hands, faces and feet. Now's a good time to tell you, right? After you've worked so hard to create your own! I know that you'll eventually thank me for the ex-

---

WHAT YOU'LL NEED FOR THESE PROJECTS:

- Polymer clay in your choice of brands and colors
- Kneading medium, such as Mix Quick
- FIMO gloss lacquer
- Cornstarch or baby powder
- Acrylic paint:
  - blue
  - black
  - brown
  - white
  - red
- Pink makeup blush or chalk
- 4 seed beads (eyes for Leprechaun and St. Nick)
- 2 small bottles for armatures
- Heavy-gauge wire (such as coat-hanger wire)
- What A Character Push Molds (optional):
  - Leprechaun—1 and 13
  - Clowns—1, 4 and 13
  - St. Nick—10 and 11
- Toothpicks
- China teacup (for Leprechaun)
- Aluminum foil
- Eleven 2″ eyepins (for marionette)
- Black thread (for marionette)
- Colored telephone wire (for clowns)
- Knife
- Rolling pin or pasta machine
- Assorted brushes (no. 2 and/or no. 4 filbert, no. 3 round, no. 1 liner)
- Oven
- Oven thermometer
- Needle tools (both sharp and blunt)
- Ruler
- Fabric for textures
- Sturdy brush handle or 7″-long piece of ¼″ dowel
- Round-nose pliers
- Wire cutters
- Kemper heart, star and circle pattern cutters (for clowns)

---

perience, as there is a great joy in creating a character that is totally yours. But sometimes you may not have the time or the patience to do it all. That's when the push molds are terrific. I used the What a Character Push Molds produced by American Art Clay Co., Inc. (and designed by me) for the models, but you can use any ceramic or plastic mold (available in craft and hobby stores). Of course, you can also sculpt your own faces for these designs.

USING READY-MADE ACCESSORIES

The leprechaun illustrates the principle that your sculpture will look more impressive if you add it to an existing object, like the teacup. Think of all the things that will fit safely into a hot oven, such as wood, stones, shells, pottery, metal and glass. I frequently visit rummage and antique sales where I pick up marvelous utensils into which to build my people. One of my favorites was a sewing machine thief, designed around old sewing machine parts.

Leonard the Leprechaun

I was just ready to make a cup of tea when the phone rang. It was my mother wanting me to pick her up some bananas for the salad that she needed for club. I hurried out the door, glancing longingly at the hot water in the cup. When I returned an hour later, there was a funny-looking scum covering the cooled water and little wet footprints across the counter. If I didn't know better, I would swear that a Wee One had come visiting! Just in case, I threw out the water and started with a fresh cup.

STEP 1   FACE

Condition the clay so that it is very smooth and moderately soft. Roll clay into a round ball, then into a very short cone shape, with the point of the cone the same size as the end of the nose. Brush mold with baby powder or cornstarch. Shake out excess. Place point of cone into nose of mold and push firmly. The mold doesn't have to be full. In fact, you can get interesting variations by using just a little clay for a tiny face or a lot for a larger face. Don't let clay shift or you will get double features. Pull face straight out from mold so as not to mar nose. If the nose is flat, the tip of the cone didn't reach the very tip of the nose in the mold. Try again with a smaller point on the cone.

STEP 2   HANDS

Roll a smooth clay rope slightly narrower than the width of the mold. Flatten hand area slightly, then pull out one side to begin to shape thumb. Brush mold with powder or cornstarch. Press hand into mold, being sure to move clay into the thumb area. Don't fill quite to edges. Use your thumb to press an indentation into the palm area. Remove hand from mold. Smooth edges. To shape wrist, roll and stretch it between your fingers. Cut between fingers if you desire. If you need a smaller hand, try filling the mold with less clay.

Roll a ¾" ball of flesh clay. Press over toothpick, flattening the front of the ball. Press face over the front of the ball. Set aside.

STEP 3   ARMATURE

Fill an old teacup half full of crumpled foil. (Check yard sales, antique shops and flea markets for single teacups.) Make a 2"-tall armature from crumpled foil. Insert a toothpick into center.

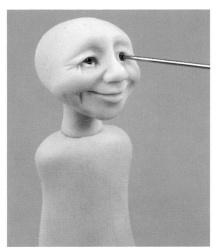

STEP 4 DETAILING THE FACE

Remove clay head from its toothpick and press onto the neck. Blend chin into neck. Deepen lines in face with a needle tool. Pick up a seed bead with the needle tool and press it into the eye, pressing it slightly deeper than the eyelid. Mark the corners of the eye with the needle tool to make an almond-shaped eye. Use the needle tool to add wrinkles to corners. Compress face slightly between forehead and chin; this will make his eyelids crinkle around his eyes.

Cover shoulders of armature with a layer of clay skin. Add a neck over the end of the toothpick.

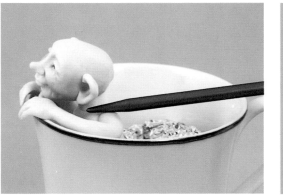

Position Leonard's hands over the brim of the teacup. Add blush to his cheeks, knuckles and elbows.

STEP 5 ARMS

Make arms approximately 2″ long. Blend arms into shoulders with a rolling motion of the needle tool. Smooth with your finger. Add ears, referring to page 28.

STEP 6 HAIR

For hair, press a layer of red-orange clay onto his head, following the beard and hairline. Use a needle tool to score swirls and lines into the hair.

STEP 7 BUBBLES

Lay a thin, white, clay sheet over the foil in the cup. Roll various sizes of clay balls and drop over surface.

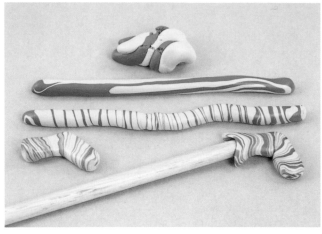

STEP 8   SOCKS

These clothes are easy ones to practice on because they don't have to fit! His socks are made by mixing together two colors of clay (your choice). Roll this marbled mix into a rope, then twist it by rolling the ends of the rope in opposite directions. Cut a sock-sized piece and shape it. Hollow out the top half. Press with fabric for texture, then lay onto saucer.

STEP 9   SHOES

The basic shape for the shoes is the same as the shoes in chapter five. Add the sole and then a wedge heel. Press a strap across the top. Add a gold buckle made from a skinny rope folded into four sides. Use a blunt edge to press wrinkles around the pointed toes.

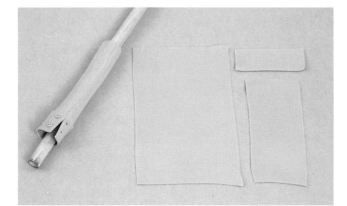

STEP 10   SHIRT

For the shirt, cut, from flattened clay, a 2″ × 1½″ rectangle, two 1½″ × 1″ rectangles for sleeves and a narrow strip for each cuff. Press with fabric for texture. To keep sleeve from collapsing when you make the seam, lay edge of sleeve over dowel, then overlap opposite side. Press on cuff. Cut in buttonholes and add small balls for buttons.

Lay large shirt piece over cup handle. Press sleeves onto shirt.

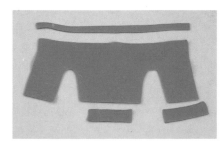

STEP 11   PANTS

Cut pants pieces from a flattened sheet of clay, using pattern on next page. Press with fabric for texture.

Place edge of seam over a dowel, as you did for the shirt sleeve, then overlap seams, matching letters. Wrap a band around each leg and the waist, keeping pants on the dowel. Cut in buttonholes and press on tiny gold balls for buttons. Lay onto saucer.

Patterns

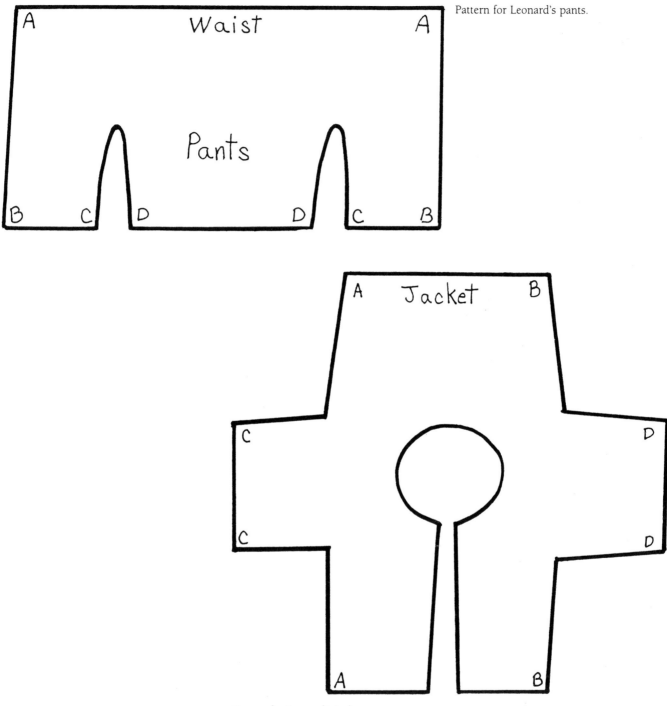

Pattern for Leonard's pants.

Pattern for Leonard's jacket.

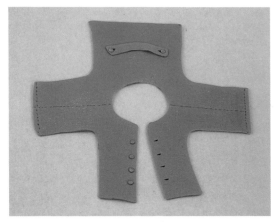

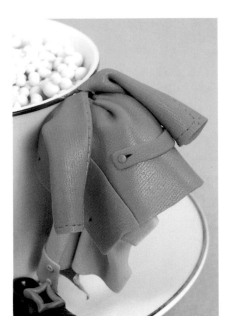

Overlap seams by matching letters, the same as you did for the shirt and pants. Draw in stitch lines. Lay jacket over shirt on cup handle.

STEP 12   JACKET

Cut jacket from a piece of flattened clay, using pattern on previous page. Press with fabric. Add belt, buttons and buttonholes.

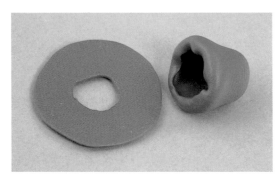

◄ STEP 13   HAT

To make hat, make a 2"-wide pancake. Cut out center. Hollow the center of a ¾"-diameter ball. Turn under edges and press over brim. Press with fabric for texture.

STEP 14   BAKING ►

Lay hat over jacket on handle. Bake in oven according to manufacturer's directions. Let cool before removing.

When cool, use an almost dry brush to lightly stroke on eyebrows. Glaze soap bubbles with gloss lacquer. At the last minute, my son-in-law suggested that I add the rubber ducky—so he was baked separately and then added. He's shaped from solid yellow clay with an orange clay beak and tiny black clay balls for eyes. I thought it was a cute idea.

Jilly and Willy the Clowns

Jilly and Willy don't have any notion of the concept of subtle and subdued. The word *clash*, when it refers to clothes, is irrelevant to them. Their mission is fun—and the more the merrier. They can often be found at hospitals or nursing homes doing some of their silly magic tricks.

A clown is a wonderful excuse to play with a riot of color. These designs are also a good way to use up all of your odds and ends of leftover color.

USING FOUND ARMATURES

A third shortcut to making clay figures is using found armatures (as opposed to "made" armatures). Search in your pantry or craft cupboard for people-shaped items that could double as an armature for your characters. These armatures can inexpensively fill up the bulk in the center of your characters. They can also provide image-enhancing weight and stability. An example for this category is the salad dressing bottle that "centers" my St. Nick. I never had to prop him or worry about him tipping in the oven, and I like the way he feels when I lift him—just enough weight. (For some reason, lightweight translates into cheap in my mind.)

The smaller bottles for the clowns were a challenge, as I didn't want them to end up looking like dumb old covered bottles. The bottles allowed me to take exactly the same ideas and make two very different people. An added advantage of using odds and ends for your characters' insides is that it keeps your shapes and ideas fresh.

A clothespin would be another good found armature, especially for creating multiple characters that are exactly the same size. This is good for production work or for group work where you all want to use the same pattern. One precaution on using wood: Leave a vent space at the bottom where any moisture in the wood can escape.

STEP 1   ARMATURES

Choose two bottles that resemble people. Mine, one skinny and one fat, are 3¾″ and 4¼″ tall. To make a support for the head, cut a wire slightly more than twice the height of the bottle. Bend it in half, loop the top and insert it into the bottle. Support with foil if necessary.

STEP 2   HEADS

Cover the loop with a small flattened ball of clay, just as you did for the leprechaun. Add a neck and shoulders if needed. Make push mold faces and press over the ball. Blend neck area.

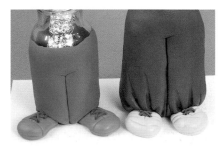

STEP 3   LEGS AND SHOES

Cover the bottom half of each bottle with a thick layer of clay. Make clay slightly thicker in the middle, near the inseam of the legs.

This allows you to sculpt the pant legs slightly. Cut the center line, then smooth away from this line to make a slight beveled edge. Press with fabric for texture. Use a blunt needle tool to press in gather marks at the base of the fuller pants. To make a space into which to press shoes, press two indentations into base of pants with your thumb. Make large shoe shapes and long skinny shoe-strings. How big? It's up to you. Just remember, big is never too big for a clown. Press in shoestring holes, then lay strings between marks. Add a tie to each. (Refer to chapter five if you need help.)

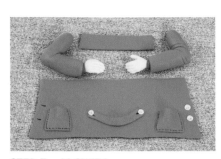

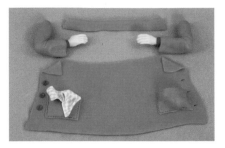

STEP 5   JACKETS

Cut pieces for the jacket, using the techniques learned in chapter seven for measuring clothes to fit. Add whatever details you like to the jackets. Make push mold hands to place into the sleeves.

STEP 4   SHIRTS

From a sheet of flattened clay, cut a shirt piece that will cover the front of each clown. Lay in place, stretching edges to fit. You needn't cover the back. Lay on a strip for the belt.

Position jackets on figures, adding the large piece first and then pressing on the sleeves. Add the collar last. Don't make the jacket clay too thin or too tight on the back of the jar. The clay seems to shrink slightly, which is especially noticeable if the clay is thin. I have had very thin clay crack during baking when placed over rigid surfaces.

STEP 6   TRIMMINGS

Blush cheeks. Add trims as desired. To Willy, I added a big bow made from some millefiori cane slices that were pressed all over the surface of a flat sheet of clay. (See page 37 for the bow pieces.) His hair is made of thin strips of clay I curled between my fingers.

Jilly's clothes are decorated with little cutout appliques made with Kemper pattern cutters. These were just cut and then pressed in place.

The hats are made from a flat pancake with a hollowed-out crown. The millefiori slices and cutouts are baked onto the wires. Make a hole in the hats to place the wires in, but don't add them until everything is baked. Once the clay is hard, you can curl, cut and adjust the wires as desired.

STEP 7   BAKING

Place the hats on their heads, then bake the figures according to manufacturer's directions. Let cool in oven.

STEP 8   PAINTING THE FACES

The hardest thing about these little guys is painting their faces. There is no trick except to go slowly and not have too much paint on your brush. Paint all of the white areas first, then add the features, using the picture as a guideline.

St. Nick

I'll let you in on a secret. St. Nick doesn't intend to give this little marionette to anyone. He had so much fun making it that he decided to keep it for his own toy chest. You did know that St. Nick had his own stash of toys, didn't you? Only someone who really loves toys himself would get such a kick out of giving them away year after year after year.

STEP 1   THE ARMATURE AND FACE
Choose a tall, full-bottomed bottle. This one is 8½″ tall. If you don't like to condition clay, choose a smaller bottle, as this St. Nick took almost seven 2-ounce packages of red clay.

Stuff top with foil. Add push mold face, being sure to deepen wrinkle lines to add character. Add seed bead eyes. Notice how his eyelids crinkle around the seed beads. You can use a brush to smooth and position the eye area. Apply blush to his cheeks and nose. Press on shoulders. The clay won't want to stick to the glass, but press firmly.

STEP 2   CLOTHES
Cover the bottom of the bottle with a red clay pancake.

Cut a sheet of clay tall enough to reach from waist to feet and wide enough to go halfway around with some room to spare for gathers. Press with fabric for texture. Add a twisted-clay belt.

Lay St. Nick on a clay sheet and cut around his outline to make a piece large enough to cover his chest. Leave enough room for a turned-under hem, which will make him look like he has a belted waist. None of this may end up showing under his beard, but one never knows!

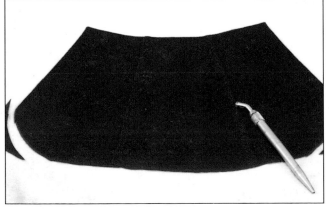

STEP 3   ROBE

To make the robe, cut three pieces that are each big enough to go one-third of the way around him. When these are seamed together, they will be plenty big enough to allow for graceful folds. Be sure to cut the pieces so that they are narrower at the top. Overlap seams. Round corners. Cut in stitch marks. Here I am using an architectural tool called a *poncing wheel* to roll in little stitch marks.

To make fur trim, roll a long white rope. Press flat, then lay trim over edge of robe. Press with a rubber stamp to create an embossed pattern (first brush the stamp with baby powder to keep it from sticking).

Fit robe around St. Nick's shoulders.

STEP 4   THE FIRST BAKE
STEP 4   THE FIRST BAKE

I stopped at this point and baked St. Nick so I would be able to concentrate on the next steps without worrying about wrecking his robe. It isn't essential, but it makes it so much easier to add the beard and hair.

Use your fingers to create soft folds around the robe. A brush can be used to lift and place folds without leaving harsh marks. Make sleeves, hollowing them to the elbow. Add trim around sleeves. Make hands from a push mold, not quite filling the mold to make smaller hands. Press hands and arms in place. Position hands so they will hold the marionette.

Cut the hood, using the pattern on the next page. Add fur trim to the top edge. Overlap the right-bottom corner over the left-bottom corner to create a little funnel-shaped hood. Place hood seam against back of neck, with hood hanging down back.

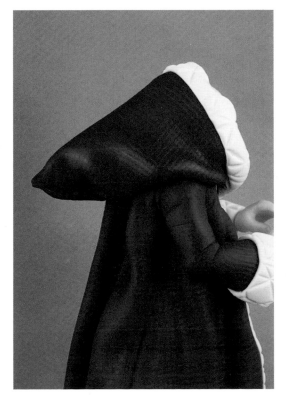

Now pull ends around and under chin.

Patterns

Hood

Add fur trim here

Pattern for St. Nick's hood.

Marionette diagram.

STEP 5 HAIR AND BEARD

Press flat pieces of white clay over the hair and beard line.

Layer on strips of curled clay, starting with the bottom layers. Adding a little superglue under the mustache and eyebrows will help them adhere.

STEP 6 THE FINAL BAKE

Bake at the highest and longest temperature recommended by the manufacturer. I usually add at least fifteen minutes with these large St. Nick's because of the bulk. Let cool in oven.

The puppet is simple, but there are lots of pieces. Follow the diagram for placement of the eyepins. Notice that a rounded end is embedded into the body, each hand and each shoe so that it won't accidentally pull out. The eyepins are baked into the pieces, then cut to size and shaped after the pieces have cooled. To make rods, roll two ropes slightly shorter than the eyepins. Thread an eyepin through each rope with the ends protruding. Flatten ropes, one on top of the other like a *T*, then bake. After baking, bend the eyepins down.

Follow diagram to string the puppet.

Problems and Solutions

The following problems are those that have come up most frequently during my clay classes. Often the student will know that something is wrong, but will not be able to actually see what is causing the character to look awkward or amateurish. To help you learn to see, and thus perceive, the problems, I have created specific examples to illustrate each point. I will then give suggestions for solving the problem.

If your work looks like some of these examples, be comforted in knowing that you are not alone! As with any long-distance diagnosis, I need to give the routine disclaimer: There is no guarantee that your specific situation will be addressed, or that my suggestions will fix it to your satisfaction. But, I do hope that this section will be of benefit to you. I wish I had had it when I was starting out in 1979.

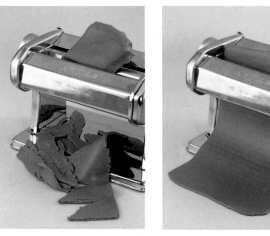

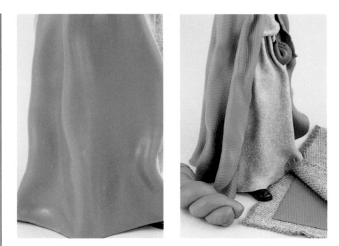

PROBLEM: Crumbly clay

The clay crumbles when it is run through the pasta machine, even though it is well conditioned and pliable.

SOLUTION: Usually this happens because the clay pancake is too thick to force between the rollers. You need to flatten it to less than ¼″ thick before you roll it through. It can also happen if your clay is too cold or too dry. If your clay crumbles, check the thickness first; then, if it still crumbles, rework it to be sure that it is warm and flexible. The last resort is to add more softener, such as Mix Quick, Friendly Clay Super Softener or Super Sculpey. Be careful not to add too much softener, as sticky clay is harder to control. You'll develop a feel for your ideal clay texture as you continue to learn and experiment.

PROBLEM: Flawed surface

The clay flattened just fine, but the surface is flawed with pits and bubbles. It also has an unattractive plastic shine.

SOLUTION: The clay surface will look pitted and bubbly if the clay is inadequately conditioned. Be sure you thoroughly knead and twist as you mix in order to have all parts uniformly pliable. If the clay feels warm, but still rolls out unevenly, add a softener. Pressing the surface with fabric to add texture will camouflage imperfections and cut the plastic shine.

I most frequently get bubbles when I have rolled out a sheet and then re-roll the scraps. There seem to be trapped bubbles between the layers. In this case, I twist the clay to break up the layers, then flatten it and run it through the pasta machine ten to twenty times, always keeping the fold at the top.

Draping

PROBLEM: Cracks

The sheets of clay crack when you try to press in wrinkles and folds.

SOLUTION: Was the clay cold when you tried to fold it? It's very risky to roll out sheets ahead of time with the idea that you will position them later. It's best to roll and then position the folds immediately. Don't come back the next day and expect to do just a few quick additional folds here and there. You're asking for trouble.

Also, if you are using a stiffer clay, you need to be gentle as you press in the folds. They do have a tendency to crack. You may want to mix in one of the softer clays or a kneading medium. The softer brands of clay will remain pliable longer than the stiffer ones.

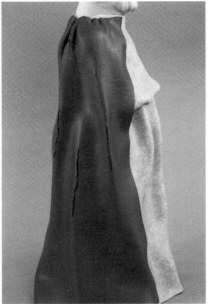

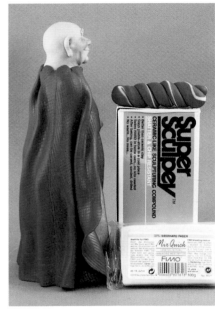

PROBLEM: Thin, stretched sheets

The sheets of clay stretched too thin as you worked with them, especially at the shoulder area. The folds and gathers droop.

SOLUTION: I'm guessing that you rolled the clay too thin for the consistency of the brand you are using. Soft clays must be rolled thicker than stiff ones, in order to give them more body. This is a tough call, as thin sheets drape so beautifully, but your first consideration needs to be the stability and durability of your sculpture: Polymer clay artists need to demonstrate that their works will last over a period of years. So don't get it too thin! That shoulder area is a critical one, as it must support the weight of the heavy arm and sleeve. I add stability here with raw-clay shoulder pads. See instructions for this technique in the Studious Stan project in chapter five.

Sleeves and Arms

PROBLEM: Flat, unrealistic sleeves

The sleeve looks like a giant finger flattened it; the texture is different at the top of the sleeve than it is at the bottom.

SOLUTION: Probably a giant finger did flatten it. Yours. Ignore the texture for now, and use your fingers to round the sides of the sleeve so that it really looks like there is an arm in there. Now press with fabric to replace the texture. View it from all angles to see that it looks natural. It also helps to look at your own sleeves in the mirror so that you have an idea of what an arm inside clothes really looks like.

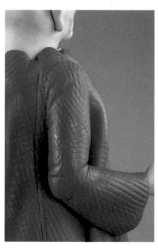

PROBLEM: Arms too long or too short

SOLUTION: There are a few basic rules to remember when measuring arms:

1. On an average adult, the elbows come to the waist.

2. On an average adult, the wrist comes to the top of the leg.

3. On an average adult, the fingers reach one-third of the way between the crotch and the knee.

I keep using the word *average* because I want to stress that these are just guidelines. Since we don't really want to create average characters, we can give ourselves permission to break the rules. However, by knowing the rules we have more control over the end results. Jonathan Andrew, the tiny tailor, has long arms in the first picture, short ones in the second and average ones in the third. Which arms look best to you?

Fingers and Hands

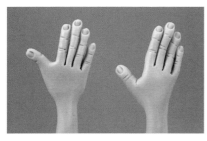

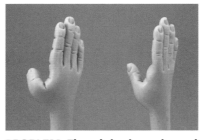

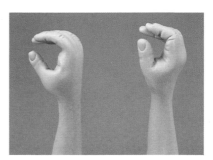

PROBLEM: Thumb in wrong position

Look at the hand at the left side of the picture. Now look at your own hand. See how the clay thumb is cut to the same line as the fingers—halfway down the hand? It should be all by itself at least three-quarters of the way down the hand, as shown in the hand on the right.

SOLUTION: Cut the thumb line a little farther down the hand, then pull and push the thumb into its lower position. You may then have to trim off the end of the thumb to make it shorter. Check out the length of your own thumb in relation to your pointer finger. My thumb ends just above the line where my pointer finger starts.

PROBLEM: Thumb looks awkward

The hand on the left looks awkward because it *is* awkward to hold your thumb in that position. You very seldom bend just the first joint of your thumb. Look at your own hand and bend your thumb to touch your little finger. See how the whole side of your hand moves when your thumb moves?

SOLUTION: Look at the palm of your own hand to see where the lowest of the three main lines cuts diagonally across your hand. That line is where you want the hand to bend. Use a knife to lightly score that line on the palm side of the clay hand so that it will be easier to bend the thumb. Now bend the thumb *and* the clay that is below the thumb. Smooth the resulting uneven surface by stroking and smudging gently with your finger.

PROBLEM: No bones in the hand

The hand at the left looks more like a bird claw, doesn't it? When the fingers bend, the bends need to correspond with the bones inside of the fingers.

SOLUTION: First look at your own hand to see where the knuckle line really is. It *isn't* right at the bottom of each finger; it is slightly lower than that. Pick the corresponding line on your little character's hand, then softly bend it at that point. Now stroke the clay toward, then away, toward and then away from that line. Gradually a knuckle ridge will build up at that line. Soften it into slight ridges with a blunt needle tool and the clay-brush tool. If you are going to bend the fingers, bend them only at the joint lines. On these little hands, I usually only bend at the knuckles and the first joint.

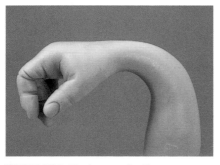

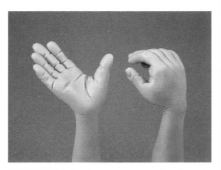

PROBLEM: No bones in the arm

This is exaggerated, but it is easy to have this happen on a sculpture. Where does the wrist bend, anyway? There is a lack of decisiveness here.

SOLUTION: Look at your own hand and wrist and watch the angles when you bend them in different directions. Now find the corresponding point on your character's hand and bend it there so that there is a definite point where the hand ends and the arm begins. The angle of the wrist is wonderfully expressive, so experiment with different angles. Smooth the wrist and add some wrinkles to make it look natural.

Facial Features

OVERALL PROBLEM: Not cute

How else can I say it? This poor little darling has a multitude of problems. Well, here's our chance to do plastic surgery. But we'll have to do it just one step at a time. As we work through these solutions, notice that solving one problem sometimes creates another.

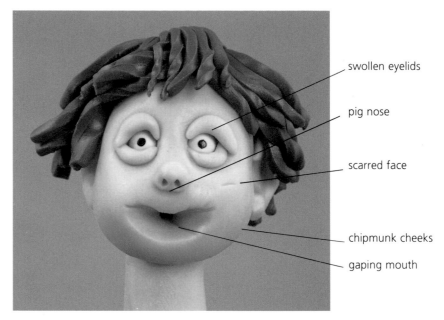

swollen eyelids

pig nose

scarred face

chipmunk cheeks

gaping mouth

SOLUTION TO: Pig Nose and Scarred Face

The first thing to do is fix that nose and those scratch marks. To fix the nose, use a needle tool and the claybrush to return the nose to its original shape. Now put the nostrils *on* the line where the nose meets the face. If you leave a space between the nostrils and the face, it will look like a pig snout.

On a simple face like this, every mark shows. Roll a blunt needle tool over the inside of the mouth to make it smooth. Then pat and brush smooth the corners and the cheeks. If you need bifocals to see, put them on! There's no room for vanity when creating helpless little souls who are depending on you for their outlook on life.

SOLUTION TO: Gaping Mouth

Why leave a mouth open so wide if it adds nothing to the character? Close it up! Do so by pushing upward gently with your thumb. Do this gradually or you will leave a big fingerprint. Lots of small pushes and pats will do the trick. Concentrate especially on the corners. Look in the mirror and make faces at yourself. It helps! (Notice that although the mouth isn't gaping anymore, the character still lacks expression.)

SOLUTION TO: No Expression

The mouth is too flat. Add some dimension by pressing into the corners with a large, blunt needle tool or similar shape. This simulates cheeks and dimples. (OK, nice smile—but look at those gouges!)

SOLUTION TO: Gouges at Cheek Corners

Soften the resulting gouges in the corners of the mouth with the claybrush tool. Lots of short, gentle brushstrokes will do the trick. A little waterless hand cleaner on the brush will speed up the process. Be careful though, as it will get sticky.

SOLUTION TO: Swollen Eyelids

This poor dear has been eating way too much salt! Remove those eyelids and make smaller ones, *much* smaller ones. Flatten them slightly before you position them. Use a brush to do final positioning so as not to leave marks. Be sure that the upper eyelids are the proper size to look as if they could really blink up and down. Now that the eyelids are smaller, I have room to color in more of the eye. If your character has a sun-dazed expression like the one in the preceding pictures, try enlarging the pupils.

SOLUTION TO: Chipmunk Cheeks

This may or may not be a problem for you, depending on how you view your character. If you want the figure to look light and elfish, chipmunk cheeks won't do. I removed the model's head from her neck and smoothed some of the cheek clay from under her chin toward the back of her head, where I trimmed it off. I also tilted her head slightly to the right to give her a whimsical look.

PROBLEM: Smudged paint

Unsteady hands or too much paint on the brush can lead to messy or smudged eyes.

SOLUTION: After all these years, I still approach eye painting with caution. One little blob does show, and it can happen anytime. If you mess it up totally, wash it off quickly before it sets. Washing won't hurt the polymer clay. If you get the eyebrows too thick or if just one line goes out of round, let it dry. Once dry, use a round wooden toothpick to scrape off the offending lines.

Now isn't our character much cuter?

Proportions

PROBLEM: Head is too big or too small

SOLUTION: When creating caricatures, body proportion isn't terribly important, as it is a mood and a personality rather than total body realism that you are trying to impart. However, if you are doing dollhouse miniatures or realistic portraits of people, it is important that the character's proportions are to scale. In the examples, my two medieval wandering storytellers show two different body proportions. Sir Garth of Bentwood (at left) looks thick and short, but strong. His friend and fellow traveler on the road, Sir Malcolm of Shilo (on the right) looks tall and thin.

When we place these two side by side, however, we see that they are actually the same height. It is the size of their heads and the resulting body proportions that cause them to look tall or short.

A common way to measure proportions is by the number of heads tall that the character is. The heads for these two were made by using push molds, so it was relatively easy for me to make duplicate heads for the purpose of measuring. Sir Malcolm measures almost eight heads tall, which is average for an adult male, while Sir Garth measures only six heads tall.

In this picture, I compare Malcolm, who is almost eight heads tall, with Jonathan Andrew, who is only five heads tall. Both look like they could fit into the same "Once upon a time . . ." story, even though they are of very different heights.

The same is true of Sir Garth and the Pumpkin Tramp in this picture. Once again, both are made from the same face mold, though each is custom sculpted a bit. The Pumpkin Tramp's short size requires a tiny body and short arms and legs in order for him to look "normal" to our eye. It may be useful at this point to consider proportions in cartoon drawings, such as Ziggy or Calvin. Can you picture them with their short little bodies and big heads? Our eye is used to seeing exaggerated body proportions if the character looks whimsical or cartoonish. This usually means being drawn with, among other things, a larger head.

In this picture, the center character, Sir Malcolm, is eight heads tall. Jonathan Andrew, on the right, is five heads tall; the size of his head still makes him fit in as a companion of Sir Malcolm—he's just a little short, that's all. The little St. Nicholas on the left, however, looks misplaced. This is because he is small all over. His tiny head is proportionate to his own body, but not to the other two in the picture. Just like Sir Malcolm, he is eight heads tall, but his head is much smaller than Malcolm's. This makes him look like a miniature St. Nicholas, which, come to think of it, is what he is.

When I compare the body proportions of my clay characters, I am drawn to the ones that are five to six heads tall. They seem more whimsical and more expressive to me; experiment to see what proportions you prefer.

Breakage

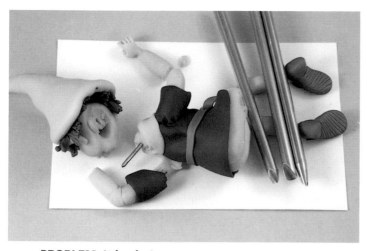

I intended him to look like this, but I neglected to prop him at all his weak points.

I had baked the armature so that it was hard. During this stage I had propped the neck on a ball of foil.

PROBLEM: It broke!

SOLUTION: Yes, breakage does happen, and it surprises me every time. Some breakage is due to improper handling. There isn't much you can do about this. If bent too far or dropped too hard, polymer clay will break. Other breakage is due to improper use. The primary reasons are:

1. **Underbaking.** If polymer clay is baked too short a time or at too low a temperature, or both, it will be very fragile. In general, I bake at the longest time and the highest temperature recommended on the clay package. Then I cool in the oven for added time. If the piece is very large or very intricate, I bake after each layer is added so that, by the final bake, I am sure that each stage is thoroughly baked.

2. **Weak Clay.** Some polymer clays are not designed for creating intricate, durable statues. If a clay is marketed for beginners and children, it may not be appropriate to use for your masterpiece.

3. **Inadequate Propping in the Oven.** Yes, it does still happen to me! I was devastated when I opened the oven this winter to see this—seven pieces that looked like garbage when I anticipated one wonderful whole. As soon as I saw it I knew what had happened. So I glued him together and recreated the steps as a lesson and example.

Then I had built the rest of his body, including a very large and heavy head. Because his arms were soft clay and too weak to support his head, I propped his legs (which at this stage were baked and very firm) with some heavy fingernail tools. This propping worked well while I was working on him. But somehow I neglected to consider that when the clay got hot in the oven, the legs would be very weak at the knee joints. They would just give way and collapse, which is what they did.

What I should have done is prop his head and his chest—or better yet, I should have designed him with a strong wire armature through his arms, like Grandpa has in chapter seven.

Discouraging? Yes, sometimes. But there are many rewards. And all of this trial and error is part of what keeps the whole art of creating with polymer clay so interesting—there's so much to remember, so much to learn, and so many ideas yet to try. Here's to the adventure. . . . I wonder what's around that next corner?

RESOURCES

The world of polymer clay is continually expanding. It's impossible to list all of the related companies and their materials, but following are those that have been instrumental in my career as a polymer clay artist.

ORGANIZATIONS

The National Polymer Clay Guild
1350 Beverly Road, Suite 115-345
McLean, VA 22101
A networking opportunity for polymer clay enthusiasts. Annual membership fee entitles one to receive newsletters full of the latest information and tips.

MANUFACTURERS OF POLYMER CLAY

American Art Clay Co., Inc.
4717 W. Sixteenth Street
Indianapolis, IN 46222-2598
Manufacturer of Friendly Clay and Friendly Clay Millefiori Canes. Also sells FIMO, tools and educational supplies.

Eberhard Faber GmbH
P.O. Box 1220
D-92302 Neumarkt/Germany
Telephone: 09181/43 0-0
Fax: 09181/4 30-222
Manufacturers of FIMO and FIMO Soft.

Polyform Products Co.
1901 Estes Avenue
Elk Grove Village, IL 60007-5415
Telephone: (847) 427-0020
Fax: (847) 427-0426
Manufacturers of Granitex, ProMat, Sculpey, Sculpey III and Super Sculpey.

T+F GmbH
RosenaustraBe 9
P.O. Box 30 12 36
D-63274 Dreieich/Germany
Telephone: (0 61 03) 6 27 06
Fax: (0 61 03) 6 54 62
Manufacturers of Cernit.

WHOLESALE/RETAIL RESOURCES

Accent Import-Export, Inc.
P.O. Box 4361
Walnut Creek, CA 94596
Telephone: (510) 827-2889
Fax: (510) 827-0521
Specializes in wholesale FIMO, FIMO Soft and KaleidoKane Classic Millefiori Canes.

The Clay Factory
P.O. Box 460587
Escondido, CA 92046-0598
Telephone: (619) 741-3242
Fax: (619) 741-5436
Specializes in wholesale/retail Cernit, Granitex, ProMat, Sculpey, Super Sculpey, Sculpey III, tools and educational materials.

Dee's Delights, Inc.
3151 State Line Road
Cincinnati, OH 45052
Telephone: (513) 353-3390
Fax: (513) 353-3933
Specializes in dollhouse and miniature supplies, FIMO, FIMO Soft, Sculpey, Super Sculpey, tools and educational supplies. Wholesale only.

Handcraft Designs, Inc.
63 East Broad Street
Hatfield, PA 19440
Telephone: (215) 855-3022
Fax: (215) 855-0184
Specializes in wholesale/retail Cernit, tools and educational materials.

Kemper Tools and Doll Supplies
13595 12th Street
Chino, CA 91710
Telephone: (909) 627-6191
Fax: (909) 627-4008
Specializes in tools, pattern cutters and Cernit. Wholesale/retail.

Perfect Touch
P.O. Box 2422
Brenham, TX 77834-2422
Telephone: (409) 830-8167
Specializes in handmade metal-tipped and wood-carved tools for the doll artist and miniaturist. Retail only.

Wee Folk Creations
18476 Natchez Avenue
Prior Lake, MN 55372
Telephone: (612) 447-3828
Fax: (612) 447-8816
Specializes in Cernit, Granitex, FIMO, FIMO Soft, ProMat, Sculpey, Super Sculpey, tools and educational supplies. Wholesale/retail.

Visual Image Printery
215 North Grove Street
Anaheim, CA 92806
Telephone: (714) 632-3491
Fax: (714) 632-3953
Specializes in Six Cubed Art Tool (large cubed rubber stamp), rubber stamps and art supplies. Wholesale/retail.

BOOKS/VIDEOS

Carlson, Maureen. *FIMO Folk* (and four other titles). Hot Off the Press, Inc., 1250 NW Third, Canby, OR 97013.

Carlson, Maureen. *Mug Dwellers and Wee Folk* videotape series (and four other titles). Wee Folk Creations, 18476 Natchez Avenue, Prior Lake, MN 55372.

Hamm, Jack. *Drawing the Head & Figure.* Perigee Books, The Putnam Publishing Group, 200 Madison Avenue, New York, NY 10016. 1963.

Oroyan, Susanna. *Fantastic Figures.* C&T Publishing, P.O. Box 1456, Lafayette, CA 94549. 1994.

Redman, Lenn. *How to Draw Caricatures.* Contemporary Books, Inc., 180 North Michigan Avenue, Chicago, IL 60610. 1984.

Roche, Nan. *The New Clay.* Flower Valley Press, Rockville, MD. 1991.

INDEX